LIFE HACKS FOR HARD TIMES

27 PROVEN AND PRACTICAL TOOLS TO GET UNSTUCK AND WIN AT LIFE

CHRISTIE HENSLER

Life Hacks for Hard Times by Christie Hensler

Published by MAXPotential, LLC
174 Rainbow Drive #7460
Livingston, TX 77399-1074

www.LifeHacksForHardTimes.com

This information is being provided to you for educational and informational purposes only. It is being shared to provide general information and as a self-help tool for your own use. It is not to be substituted for the advice of licensed professionals of any kind. This information is to be used at your own risk based on your own judgment. The stories in this book are used with permission and all names have been changed to protect their anonymity. For my full Disclaimer, please go to
https://www.maxpotential.coach/disclaimer.

Cover design by Phillip Ortiz / Peel Creative
Editing by Janet Houck, Nancy Vine

ISBN: 979-8-218-05806-7

Printed in the United States of America
First Edition

DON'T MISS OUT

In order to get the most out of the book, we created a bundle of practical tools to help you get unstuck and win at life no matter where you are in life right now!

Download your FREE resources at
www.lifehacksforhardtimes.com.

DEDICATION

F or Matt, my rock. You're the one person who knows everything about me, yet still continues to selflessly love me and make me laugh every single day of my life. Thanks for choosing to show up, lock arms, and make this world a better place with me!

For my parents, who have held me with an open hand my entire life, encouraged me to go for my dreams, and unconditionally loved me through every season. Even from miles away, I know they're my biggest cheerleaders and strongest prayer warriors.

For the only constant throughout my entire life, the One who has been there through every storm, in every valley, and in the middle of every crisis. He's always been 100% faithful no matter my circumstances. He's the one who deserves all the credit for preserving my life and my purpose for such a time as this, my Creator, God.

CONTENTS

PREFACE

The future was bright. I was 19, married, and had big plans and lots of dreams! After a re-location, an underhanded house deal that cost me over $20k, and a divorce, the future wasn't looking so bright. But I was still young and had my whole life ahead of me, so I picked up the broken pieces, brushed myself off, and tried to start over. However, I made some bad choices and landed myself once again heartbroken and in the mental health institute. This time I thought - "it is time for Christie to get her act together and rebuild her life." Then came another marriage, an almost divorce, a battle with infertility and life threw me another 7-year punch in the face with a physical and mental health battle for my life.

Anxious for a fresh start and a new beginning, my family and I sold everything we owned, bought an old, but paid for, RV, and started traveling the country. This life-on-the-road adventure that we thought would be a fun thing to do for the next 6 months turned into years of "life on the road", full of challenges and obstacles. During this time, I had to figure out the basics of life (like where we would live each week), build a business on the road, beat irrational fears that plagued me for years, and take care of my family. I've had to learn to find beauty in the simple things and be content where I am while moving towards something better.

In the midst of it all, there have been some things that have kept me grounded, given me the resilience and grit to continue to get back up every time I was knocked down, and have an unshakeable joy that encompasses me throughout every valley I've crawled through and every mountain I've climbed.

As I'm invited into people's lives and stories every day of my life, I see a common thread, and that's that everyone, everywhere is going through something. Life is filled with mountains, valleys, potholes, hurdles, detours, and unexpected road closings. Sometimes we find ourselves traveling roads we never expected to travel; nonetheless, here we are, whether by choice or life's curveballs. There is always more than meets the eye and always more to the story. Maybe that's you too, friend. Maybe that smile you put on your face every day covers up the challenges and obstacles you are currently facing. Maybe you've been struggling far too long and have hope that you can get to the other side, but don't have the tools.

While I continue to live my very imperfect life every single day, I tap into the mindsets and tools in this book to empower me to be present in the moment, navigate obstacles with confidence, and find joy in my journey. I want the same for you because I learned a long time ago that if I'm waiting for perfect circumstances to enjoy my life, it will never happen. But, if I let them, the hard times can bring a depth and beauty to my life that it wouldn't have without them. My hard times can refine me and help me become the best version of myself; a version that can go to bed at night fulfilled and can make a difference in my world…one life at a time.

No matter where you find yourself reading this book, remember, your now doesn't have to be your forever. You have the power within you to overcome obstacles and enjoy life.

Thanks for coming alongside me on this journey! I'm so glad you are here!

♡ Christie

INTRO

WHY HARD TIMES?

"A diamond is a chunk of coal that did well under pressure." -Henry Kissinger

Whether or not you are going to have hard times in your life isn't the question. Hard times are inevitable for all of us. The question we should be asking ourselves is, "What am I going to do with this hard time?"

Hard times come in all different shapes and sizes. Sometimes they are consequences of our own poor decisions, and sometimes we are the victims of other people's poor decisions. Hard times can also look like worldwide crises or natural disasters. Sometimes they are brought on by toxic relationships or results of trauma we've experienced in our life. Other times, life just throws us curve balls that we didn't see coming.

Hard times happen for different reasons and, as human beings, we are built to have the power within us to survive them. Generally speaking, when a hard time comes, we realize we are stronger than we ever thought we were and have resilience we didn't even know we had.

What we lack during these hard times are the tools to be able to navigate, overcome and grow through them. There is something phenomenal that happens in us when we "grow through" and become a better version of ourselves on the other side of a difficult time, rather than just surviving it, hoping to come out on the other side at least alive. We may get out of it alive, but when we aren't intentional about growing through it, we end up broken and bitter.

In this book, you are going to hear real, raw stories of some of the hard times I've experienced in my own life. You are going to see how they came in all different shapes and sizes, but the common thread you should see throughout this entire book is how each and every one of those hard times refined me and molded me into the person I am today. We all have a choice when we face hard times in our life. We can choose to be the victim or we can choose to be the victor and use those challenges as stepping stones in our own lives, and use our own experiences to help someone else.

How To Get the Most Out of This Book

This book was intentionally written to not just inspire and encourage you, but to also give you the tangible steps to walk through whatever you are going through. The first step to get the most out of this book is to have an open mind and realize that no matter where you are right now in your life, you don't have to stay there. You can overcome and be better on the other side.

When you first read this book, I would suggest you read it from cover to cover in the order it was written. Then, I would go back and re-read the sections you need to focus on right now in your own life. This book should be referred to often and act as a user guide for "growing through what you go through". It's not meant to be a "one and done, read it and stick it on the shelf" book. Keep it somewhere handy, underline and highlight things that stand out to you, and use the tools in it to overcome hard times and enjoy your life!

This book is divided into 3 main sections:

- ➢ See
- ➢ Believe
- ➢ Do

The first section is SEE. In order to truly handle any situation you are facing, you have to know what you are really dealing with. You have to strip away all preconceived assumptions, identify the truth, and see the situation for what it really is. This has to come first before any of the other tools in this book can work. In this section, you will learn how to properly identify what's keeping you stuck, learn how to have the proper perspective, and gain the awareness you need to utilize the steps that follow.

Once you SEE things for what they really are, then you move to the BELIEVE section, which is critical, because without the right mindset and belief that you can overcome the obstacle you are facing, you have no chance. This section will explain the mindsets and belief systems you need to adopt to truly overcome and equip you to make these mindsets part of your life.

Once you SEE and BELIEVE, now you move into DOING the practical steps to change your situation for the better. Without this step, it's all just great theories. You can SEE and BELIEVE all day long, but without action and putting things in motion, nothing is going to happen (unless it's divine intervention). The tools in this section will serve you well throughout your entire life, and when used with a foundation of SEEING and BELIEVING, they will impact your life in ways you never thought possible.

In each chapter, you will find the following format:

➢ **Quote:** Relates to the topic at hand to inspire you.
➢ **Story:** Shared from my own life that will help you see how that particular Life Hack has played out in my life. It is my sincere hope that these stories inspire and empower you through your own struggles. Friend, I didn't hold anything back in this book. Some of these stories I've never told anyone before.
➢ **Key Points:** You'll find a list of key points that I've learned about the Life Hack.
➢ **How To's:** These will equip you to take action on the key points.
➢ **Checklist:** At the end of every chapter, there will be a quick checklist to recap the high points of the chapter as an easy reference for you.
➢ **Self-Coaching Questions:** Look for the bubble   in each chapter with self-coaching questions. Use these powerful questions to self-coach yourself through a particular struggle.

I can inspire and motivate you all day long, but what I really want is to equip you to win at your own life! I want to equip you to overcome whatever you have gone through in the past or are currently going through and become the person you were meant to become.

Now, let's get to it.

SEE

Your first step to getting through a hard time is acknowledging there is a problem. Then, when you look at it through the proper lens, gain awareness, and gather some options, suddenly you are filled with hope and propelled forward, believing you can and will get to the other side.

CHAPTER 1

IDENTIFY THE TRUTH

Your First Step to Getting Unstuck

"Denying the truth doesn't change the facts." - Anonymous

"If you are going to be single again, then I want a chance to date you before anyone else gets that chance." As I was separated from my husband at the time, facing the high probability of divorce, those were the words spoken to me by one of my best friends. He and I were alike in so many ways. We were both driven, highly motivated, and loved to have fun. We found opportunities and took risks every chance we got. However, the risk I was about to embark on was one I would come to regret, and one that I would pay the consequences of for years to come. Not only was I not officially divorced yet, the bigger issue was that he was still married...to one of my friends. We were both in frustrating and lifeless marriages, so we fell for each other - hard.

The thrill and excitement that came from a "new" relationship, the life we started dreaming we could have together with both our skill sets, the way we worked together, and the strong bond we shared, led us to carry on this relationship for almost a year. It was a relationship full of mistrust, lies, and manipulation, but it felt so good and so genuine. Yet, it was so screwed up, but within my broken heart, my deep longing to be seen and loved, and my desire to have a passionate relationship, I kept telling myself the truth didn't matter. As I drove him home drunk from the bars at 3am, I told myself he loved me. As I lied to his wife and my friends about where I was or what I was doing, I told myself the payoff was worth it. As I slept with a married man several hours before, I still got up and went to church the next day, acting as if "life was good and I loved Jesus". As he told me he was going to leave his wife and marry me, I foolishly believed him. Then, the following week, he told me that he was going to go to counseling with his wife to see if he could work out his marriage, but he wanted me to stay around in case it didn't. I knew this was the beginning of the end of something that should have never started in the first place.

Then came the night he met me in a parking lot so I could give him back some paperwork I had of his, and as he got out of his car and our eyes met, I noticed something on his hand that had never been there in the 5 years I had known him. His wedding ring. That was the tipping point for my broken heart and I lost it. To say I was upset is a complete understatement. My heart hurt so badly that I wanted to die that night. The rage that built inside of me led me to rip out the visors inside my car (which would later be fixed by a mechanic with shiny metal screws to hold them up and remind me of that night every single time I drove that car). That night brought a screeching halt to that relationship and led me to the hospital, which led me to the mental health ward, a place I never planned on finding myself and would have to spend the next 24 hours fighting my way out of.

It literally took me the next 10 years of my life to recover from that relationship, the consequences of my own poor decisions, and the pure grief and regret I dealt with as a result.

Why am I telling you this story? You thought you bought a book with some practical life hacks for your hard times and now you feel like you are reading a novel based on a soap opera. Hang with me. I promise I'm not writing a soap opera.

No matter what your hard time is - whether it was self-inflicted or one of life's curveballs - the very first step in getting unstuck and moving through it is you have to identify the truth of the situation. As you can see, when you and I lie to ourselves, it only puts us further in a hole that we'll one day have to dig ourselves out of. And it will take longer and be harder to recover from, the more we lie to ourselves.

Here's what I've learned about Identifying the Truth in my life:

- ➢ **It is the foundation to getting unstuck.** You must always start with the truth of where you are. No matter how screwed up the situation is, no matter how wrong you are in the situation, and no matter how much you fear what others may think, you MUST clearly state the truth - the good, the bad, and the ugly. Without it, none of the other steps in this book will serve you well because you'll be building on a broken foundation.

- ➢ **Stating the truth doesn't have to mean you are being negative.** A lot of times people think that they can't state the truth of their situation because it sounds negative or they don't want to "speak something into existence". Friends, that is completely ridiculous. If I am given a cancer diagnosis, it does me no good to go around and refuse to acknowledge I have that diagnosis. Also, me acknowledging it doesn't mean I'm accepting death, nor does it mean I'm speaking it into being - it's already there! I may as well call a spade a spade and know exactly what I am dealing with so I can deal with it. It's not either/or. You can still speak the truth and have a positive outlook on the situation. Using my example, I can view my diagnosis in two different ways (more on that in the next chapter). I can say, "I'm going to die." "There's no purpose for me here, so God's allowing me to die with this horrible disease." "Everything bad always happens to me." "I can't believe I am suffering with this." "My life is over, so I may as well give up now and throw in the towel." OR I can say, "I've been given a diagnosis, however,

5

there have been many people who have conquered this beast, and I'm going to let their stories inspire me." "I'm going to use this diagnosis to take care of my body, reevaluate my priorities, and build my resilience." I believe this is going to prepare me for the next season in my life, and I'm going to be able to help others through what I've been through." "It's going to be hard, I'm going to be scared, but I'm going to get the right support system, and I'm going to win this battle." Do you see how I can state the truth, without denying it, yet keep a positive outlook?

➢ **"Toxic Positivity" will destroy you.** Dr. Caroline Leaf, author of several books, including *Cleaning Up Your Mental Mess*, has coined the term "toxic positivity", and I love it! There is a place for positivity as well as positive affirmations in your life, but friends, denying the truth and just stating a bunch of random positive affirmations will get you nowhere if you don't truly believe what you are even chanting. I can put post-its on my mirror all day long that say, "I'm skinny and healthy!" "I look amazing!" "My body is at my optimal weight." "I am fit!" But if I'm sitting around all day in my leggings and hair in a bun, no makeup, eating Doritos and watching TV, none of that is true, nor is it going to become true. Those are just "nice words on my mirror." Now, if I am getting up at 6am and exercising every day, taking care of my body, and putting on my best self, then I'm coupling action with the positive statements and seeing those things actually happen in my life, not just wishing they would happen. You aren't fooling the people in your life with your toxic positivity, fake pictures and words on Instagram that are "impressing" everyone, while inside your life and home are falling apart. You are only fooling yourself, just like I was in my story above, and at some point, it's all going to fall apart on you because you aren't building a life on a foundation of truth. Stop being "fake positive" and start being real with yourself and watch how your life transforms in amazing ways!

How To Get It:

1. Start by asking yourself powerful questions and being honest with yourself. Powerful questions help you dig deeper below the surface of what's really going on. These are the questions you will find in the self-coaching bubbles at the end of each chapter.

2. Another method I have used is "Bust the Myth" (some of this is work done by Byron Katie - you can look up her resources for more on this).
    a) Write down what you think the truth is. Ex: It's weak for me to cry.
    b) Ask yourself, "Is this the truth?" That it's weak for me to cry.
    c) Ask yourself, "Is this 100% the truth?"
    d) Ask yourself, "What part of this is true?"
    e) Stand in your truth while you move through the pain and toward freedom in your hard situation.

3. Then, you'll need to get some Perspective, which is covered in Chapter 2, and figure out your Options, which is covered in Chapter 4.

Checklist

☐ Identifying the truth of your situation (no matter how hard or scary it feels) is your first step to getting unstuck and building a solid plan to wholeness.

☐ "Toxic positivity" and denying the truth will only put you in a deeper hole. You can speak the truth while still having a positive outlook on the situation.

☐ Ask yourself powerful questions about your situation.

☐ Be honest with yourself.

Self-Coaching Questions

- ✓ What are you afraid will happen if you speak the truth?
- ✓ What's really holding you back from being honest about your situation?
- ✓ What are you not saying right now?

CHAPTER 2

GET PERSPECTIVE

Start Looking Through a Different Lens

"Your perspective will either become your prison or your passport." - Steven Furtick

S everal years ago, life threw me a curveball I wasn't expecting, and I found myself in a literal battle for my life as anxiety, panic attacks, OCD, suicidal thoughts, depression, and irrational fears gripped my mind and my life. In hindsight, I see how I ended up there, but in the moment, it completely blindsided me. I went from having big dreams, building a business, growing a family, ready to conquer the world to curled up in a ball in the corner of my dining room unable to function or lying in bed scared to death to even get up and face the world. I lived like this for 7 very, very long years while fighting with every ounce of my being to find answers and win this war. During those 7 years, we racked up tens of thousands of dollars in debt, paying for what we thought would be solutions to my problem. I created a daunting list of bad habits and mindsets trying to control the fear and OCD, which only enabled it to control me more. I've spent years undoing those thought patterns and have fought hard for every bit of mental freedom I have to this day. I was so scared of so many things in my possession. I'm almost embarrassed to tell you that fear led me to throwing a lot of valuable things away, like my expensive smartphone, jewelry, and even my wedding ring, which was lost somewhere in that mess as well. I missed out on being present for the early years of all of my kids' lives.

In the end, my husband, Matt, and I ended up walking away from everything we spent years working for, including his engineering career, our interior-designed house, and I even lost some relationships along the way. So why am I telling you all of this? I want to show you the power of perspective. I could easily look back at this season of my life and feel immense grief, sadness, and heartache for everything I squandered and lost. Yes, I can replace stuff, but I can't ever get my kids back as babies or toddlers. I can't ever get back that time I wasted. That's one perspective. But if I take off those glasses and put on another pair with a different lens, I can look at the exact same situation and think something like this: Those years built a resilience in me that I'll carry with me for the rest of my life to navigate any other obstacles life throws my way. Those years built a depth of compassion, empathy, and character in me that I wouldn't have otherwise. Those years equipped me to be able to see others' pain, inspire and give them hope, but also give them tools to get to the other side of their own pain. Those years weren't wasted at all, they were stored up to empower me to do the work and impact the lives of the people I am here to impact.

Do you see the difference? One lens puts me in a place of regret and self-pity. The other lens puts me in a mindset of gratitude and opportunity. Same story, different lens.

Here's what I've learned about Perspective:

> ➢ **It's a powerful tool to help you identify what's really important.** What do I mean by that? So many times the hard things we go through are inconveniences, not life-altering crises. A lot of times in our moment of hardship, we think the sky is falling, when really we

just need a new car battery or the construction on the road is going to make us 15 minutes late for our appointment. Or at the time of writing this, our AC unit went out in our house in the middle of July and it's 100 degrees. As uncomfortable, sweaty and hot as I am, at the end of the day it was really just an inconvenience. Perspective will help you distinguish between what's an inconvenience and what's a life-altering crisis.

➤ **It helps you stay grounded and avoid panic mode.** During hard times, one of the things we must do is make decisions, and sometimes a lot of decisions. It's important in those decisions that we avoid panic mode, take the emotions out of the decision-making process, and stay grounded so we don't put ourselves into a bigger hardship. Perspective will do that for you.

➤ **It helps you look through a lens of everything that is right instead of everything that is wrong.** So many times, when hard times happen, it's easy to just look down and stare at the crap we are standing in. That's a natural human response. However, it's important during those hard times that we see the whole picture, that we see everything that has gone right in our lives in the past, and everything that is going right in our lives now. This allows us to look through the lens of gratitude and opportunity instead of self-pity and despair.

So, perspective sounds like an amazing tool to have in your toolbox and it is! It's one of my favorite words, hands down. But how do you grab it for your situation?

How To Get It:

1. Start with Chapter 1 - Identify the Truth - you must identify the truth of your situation - don't make your situation sound better OR worse than it actually is. Know the truth. Be honest with yourself.

2. Ask yourself, "Is this an inconvenience or a life-altering crisis?" No matter how you feel, for a moment, step out of the emotion and

answer that question. (*I'm not asking you to ignore the emotions - more on this in the Emotions Chapter 18)

3. Ask yourself, "What is going right in this situation or in my life right now?" Start from a place of gratitude. That will automatically shift your situation into proper perspective.

4. List ALL of your options in this situation. *Chapter 4 will show you exactly how to do this.

Checklist

☐ Perspective will help you distinguish and identify what's really important in your life.

☐ It's important that you use perspective to stay grounded and make decisions from a place of peace, not panic.

☐ If you are looking through a lens of everything that is wrong, you need to change your perspective lens to looking at what's right about your life.

☐ You must identify the truth of your situation like we talked about in Chapter 1. Don't skip this step.

☐ It's important that you ask yourself the powerful questions in this chapter and answer them honestly.

☐ Make sure you get a healthy perspective before you read about options in Chapter 4.

Self-Coaching Questions

✓ Am I looking at this problem through a lens of a healthy perspective?

✓ What are my options?

✓ Will this matter two years from now?

CHAPTER 3

SELF-AWARENESS

The Man in the Mirror

"Knowing yourself is the beginning of all wisdom." - Aristotle

As I found myself driving home from work with tears in my eyes…and then the next morning driving to work with tears in my eyes, I realized something had to change. At the time, I was working for a large ministry with some strict requirements, such as, I had to wear dresses and pantyhose every day. Now, you have to understand that I firmly believe pantyhose were created by the devil and I haven't worn a pair since I quit that job. I started in a position where I had to answer over 100 phone calls a day from random strangers calling in. Now don't get me wrong, I'm not at all opposed to putting someone on a newsletter list or praying for someone's sick dog, but when I started getting calls with "sick" people on the other end masturbating while on the phone with me, I was DONE with that position. I then moved to a position where I had to sit down and count numbers all day, while not talking to the person beside me. I had to ask to go to the bathroom. I hadn't done that since I was in elementary school. One day I got reprimanded for singing "Home on the Range " quietly to the co-workers beside me. I just couldn't be quiet any longer!! It was a stable job, with good benefits, and at that point in my short adult life, the best "job" I had landed. But I was miserable, so I took a look inside myself and with some self-awareness realized why I was so miserable. I was a people person, yet I was stuck staring at numbers all day and not allowed to talk. I am a person who doesn't want to be micromanaged, and here I am, having to ask to go to the bathroom and be told what I can and cannot wear. I am also a person who loves a fast-paced, think-on-my-feet environment, and nothing about what I was doing was any of that. Within two weeks, I had myself another job that I thrived at for many years.

The very first thing I did in this situation was "identify the truth"! I was miserable at this job. Yes, I was working for a ministry. Yes, some would say I was "doing God's work", but at the end of the day, I was miserable and needed to make a change. Then I looked within myself and realized WHY I felt the way I did, and it made total sense and validated the feelings I had. I then grabbed myself some options - which I'll explore with you in the next chapter - and made a decision to move me out of that miserable season and into one that I flourished in for years!

Here's what I've learned about Self-Awareness:

> **Knowing yourself is one of the most powerful tools you have.** Hard times come with a ton of emotions and stress. When you understand yourself in a very intimate way, it empowers you to handle that stress. When you know things like: what ticks you off, what your greatest fear is, what kind of things trigger you, what brings you joy, what you'll fight for no matter what, what motivates you, you set yourself up to immediately have clarity on what is causing you the most stress and elevating your emotions during your hard time. You know exactly why you are feeling some of the emotions and stress you are feeling. Your feelings are instantly validated. You no longer feel guilty or crazy for feeling the way you do.

➢ **Take the emotion out of it.** Understanding point 1 allows you to take your panic and stress level down, which will equip you to take the emotion out of it (more on this in Chapter 18 on Emotions).

➢ **Empowers you with confidence.** Because you have clarity and understanding of yourself and how this situation is affecting you, it immediately empowers you to make better decisions and move through the situation with confidence, rather than reacting to all the stress and emotions flooding your heart and mind.

How To Get It:

1. Commit to getting to know yourself better than anyone else knows you.

2. Take personality assessments and review them to gain understanding about yourself. I have used several of these assessments, and they have all helped me in different ways. You'll find links to all of these in the RESOURCES section as well.
   a) DISC - This report is the clearest and most straightforward way to understand things about yourself, like what motivates you, your greatest fear, how you react under pressure, how you communicate with others, and so on. This is the assessment I use with all of my coaching clients. You can find more information on the power of this assessment by visiting www.maxpotential.coach/disc
   b) Clifton StrengthsFinders - This report helped me tremendously to understand my top strengths that I can leverage in my own life, business, and with teams. This report has also helped me when working with teams or families so they understand how to work better together and leverage, instead of tolerating, each other's strengths (and weaknesses).
   c) Enneagram - The understanding of the Enneagram has helped me personally understand my core fears and what really drives me when my back is up against the wall, and why certain things trigger me and other things don't even faze me. This is a great tool for working together as a family unit as well. *I will say I

have had the best results for myself and my clients through taking the paid assessment - you can get those through The Enneagram Institute. I have found the free tests to not always be accurate or comprehensive.

3. Reflect on other hard times you've had in the past and ask yourself how you felt during those AND why? This will help you uncover more understanding about YOU.

4. Get others' input. Sometimes we don't always see what it's like to live on "the other side of us". We don't always see the way we come across to others or the way they see us. This is a key - *If you have people in your life who truly love you and have your best interest at heart - ask them things like, "What do you think two of my greatest strengths are?" "What do you think is one of my biggest triggers?" "What kinds of things tick me off?" "When am I at my best?"

Checklist

☐ Knowing yourself is one of the most powerful tools you have. Make it a priority in your life.

☐ Understand why your hard time is triggering the emotions inside of you so you can move forward with clarity and understanding.

☐ Step outside of the emotion of the situation, identify the truth, grab perspective and your options, then move forward intentionally and not from a place of reacting to panic or stress.

☐ Invest the time, energy, and money into taking some personality assessments and getting to know yourself better. **It will be an investment that pays you dividends for the rest of your life.**

☐ Get input from others in your life who care about you and want to see you develop into your best self.

Self-Coaching Questions

- ✓ What brings you joy?
- ✓ When are you at your best?
- ✓ What are you afraid of?
- ✓ What ticks you off?

CHAPTER 4

OPTIONS

The Power to Choose

"Everything I do is by choice. There is always another option." - Anonymous

A s I was walking toward my terminal to board my plane in Orlando, Florida, ready to head back to Pittsburgh after a long, but exciting weekend, an announcement came over the loudspeaker. "Attention passengers on Flight 473 headed to Pittsburgh - this flight has been canceled due to unforeseen circumstances. Please return to the ticket desk." My first thought was "Noooooo!" I had already pained myself to go through TSA, and I had a team of people traveling with me. Some of them needed to be at work the next morning. As we stood in the ticket counter line for nearly 2 hours (not to mention we were the third people in line), I quickly realized that the economy airline we were flying on also had "economy level" customer service. As I heard them tell the two doctors in line in front of us, who had surgeries scheduled for patients the next morning, that there was nothing they could do to get them home in time, I immediately knew I was going to have to find another option and think quickly. My mind quickly sorted all of my options, and I looked at my team and said, "I'm going to get them to refund our tickets. Then I'm going downstairs to rent us a 15-passenger van and drive us home through the night. I'll have you back home by lunchtime tomorrow." At first glance, a few of them hesitated; the last thing they wanted to do was drive 14 hours through the night home when they were already tired and ready for their own bed. But after a few minutes, they all concurred that they would go with the plan. We even had some other passengers in line wanting to know if we had some extra seats! After hours of dealing with incompetent customer service, we finally got our tickets refunded and headed down the escalator. I sent the team to grab our luggage while Matt and I went to the rental car counters. I quickly realized that grabbing a 15-passenger van from the Orlando airport at 10pm on a Sunday night might not be as simple as I originally thought. So once again, I started quickly sorting options in my head. I looked at Matt and was like, "We can rent a Penske truck with a mattress and throw everyone in the back of it." To which I got "the look". I quickly realized I better keep looking for a 15-passenger van. Finally, after the 3rd ticket counter, I secured a van! At 11pm, we all loaded our luggage in that van and began an unexpected road trip. By the time we arrived back to Pittsburgh, around 1pm the next day, we were all sleep deprived, smelled like we hadn't changed our underwear in a week, and looked like death warmed over, BUT we had a blast! We played games all night, we laughed until it hurt, and we bonded as a team in a way we would never have if we had just flown home that night. As inconvenient and hard as it was, it is a memory and story that none of us forget to this day. After all the excitement of the weekend, one of the members even said, "This was the best part of the trip!" And she was one of the ones who was hesitant to even go along with my crazy idea.

That is the power of options, friends. While I believe all of the chapters of this book are important and incredibly useful in navigating hard times, this chapter is going to be one that you will refer to over and over again. You are going to see me refer back to this chapter several times throughout this book.

Here's what I've learned about Options:

➤ **You always have more options than you think you do in any given situation.** Let's take my example above. If I were to sit down and write out all the options I had that evening at the airport, the list would have looked something like this:

- o We can sleep on the airport floor for a couple of days until they find us a flight home.
- o We can go get a hotel and extend our vacation until we get a flight home.
- o We can find a bus to get us there.
- o We can get our tickets refunded and go book a flight on a completely different airline.
- o We can grab an Uber or taxi (yes that would get expensive).
- o We can drive to another airport a couple of hours away and find a flight.
- o We can rent a van and drive ourselves home.
- o We can stay overnight in a hotel and then rent a van and drive through the day.
- o We can grab our stuff and start walking (may take a while).
- o We can rent a U-Haul and throw everyone in the back.
- o We can call someone from Pittsburgh to drive down and pick us up.

Just off the top of my head, I was able to come up with 11 options for that one scenario. Now, are they all great options? Not at all, but they are still options, which leads me to my second point.

➤ **Finding your options will help you see you have choices.** You are not stuck with just one option. A lot of times in hard situations we feel like we are stuck and can only do this one thing, and that's simply not the case. Just because you may not see any other options at the moment, doesn't mean they aren't there. This chapter will empower you to start seeing them!

Options are a key to problem-solving and decision-making. They expand your thinking to get out of your own narrow-minded, little box and get your mind to start to see the possibilities. When you start seeing the possibilities, you gain the confidence that you can solve your problem, which then empowers you to take action.

Now that you are seeing the power of options, you are probably wondering, "How do I learn this skill and implement this in my own life?"

How To Get It:

1. Grab a piece of paper and at the top write down your current problem/hard time.

2. Start listing all of your options related to the problem you wrote down. *Caution: Do NOT judge the options as you write them. Just write them down. No matter how absurd or crazy you may think they are, write them down. Remember, they are still options.

3. If your list is very short or you are struggling to think of options, find a family member, friend or someone you trust, who preferably is a big picture thinker, and get their perspective. They will be able to see options that you aren't seeing because they are outside of the situation.

4. Add their options to your list.

5. Now filter your options through the lens of your values, priorities and vision for your life. There is much more info on this in Chapter 20 on Decision-Making.

Checklist

☐ Remember, you always have more options than you think. You are never stuck.

☐ Options will equip and empower you to have the confidence to problem solve and make better decisions.

☐ It's important that you list all of your options without judging them; this will bring clarity on what you really want or don't want in the situation.

☐ Ask a friend for their perspective on your options if you are struggling to find options or even want another viewpoint.

☐ Filter your options through the lens of your values, priorities, and vision for your life to help you narrow down the list and find the best option.

Self-Coaching Questions

✓ Which of these options have I tried in the past?
✓ What were the results of those decisions?
✓ What do I really want?

BELIEVE

H aving the right mindset and belief system in place will make a huge impact in the way you overcome obstacles. The tools in this section will be what empower you to come out on the other side of your situation better than before it.

CHAPTER 5

GROWTH MINDSET

Grow Through What You Go Through

"In any given moment we have two options: to step forward into growth or step back into safety." - Abraham Maslow

I was at a crossroads in my entrepreneurial endeavors, and I needed someone to come alongside me and help me get this new business off the ground and clarify my vision and ideas. I was between two options, and I made the one that I felt in my gut was the right decision. I also made the one that was the biggest investment of my time and finances. At this point, this was the first time I invested a 5-figure amount into my own personal coaching and development, but I was betting on myself and the wisdom and experience of the coaches I was bringing alongside me. Six months later I found myself here...

I stared into the Zoom camera as my mindset coach, Sandy, asked me, "How's it going?" My response was, "Do you want to know the real truth?" Of course I knew the answer to that question, but I also had some hesitations because of the situation I was about to unfold for her. The tears began to stream down my face as I sat in my own vulnerability and told her how taken advantage of I felt, how disappointed I was, and how unvalued I felt by my other business coach, whom she was working in partnership with. I knew in that moment that I risked Sandy defending her, which would immediately destroy any credibility I felt toward Sandy, whom I loved, but it was the truth, and it needed to be spoken.

She was totally taken aback, having no idea anything was wrong in the process, because I am very good at making things happen and pushing through. Even when things are falling apart around me, no one knows, but me. So that's what I did in this situation. I realized at this moment that I should have spoken up for myself, I shouldn't have paid the full amount, and I shouldn't have allowed myself to be treated like I was treated. I was hurt and angry. My mind immediately wanted to tell me things like, "That was the dumbest decision you ever made." "You just lost a bunch of money you worked so hard for." "This is what happens when you trust people." I also started immediately questioning my gut, which has steered me right my whole life (more on that in Chapter 15), and wondering how I could have been so off to make such a horrible decision.

However, after talking through it, gaining awareness, and getting to the bottom of what was really behind my tears, Sandy helped me uncover why I gave my power away AND more importantly how to never, ever let that happen to me again. That one lesson, I have no doubt, will save me from future failures that could potentially cost me way more than 5 figures.

That day, I learned that instead of beating myself up, vowing to never take a risk again or never trust anyone again, I decided to take what seemed like a horrible, painful, and stupid decision and turn it into a valuable lesson that I'll carry with me the rest of my life; one that will protect me from far worse decisions, and one that will empower me to walk in the best version of myself without giving my power away.

Friends, that's the power of having a growth mindset over a fixed mindset.

So, what is the difference between the two mindsets? A person with a growth mindset embraces challenges, perseveres, learns from failures, and accepts criticism and feedback from others. They always have a desire to learn, believe with effort they can build new skills and abilities, and find inspiration in others' success. On the other hand, a person with a fixed mindset avoids challenges, gives up easily, and ignores feedback from others. They feel threatened by others' success. They want to see themselves as the "smartest person in the room" rather than being around people they can learn and grow from. They believe their abilities and skills can never improve and their efforts to grow are fruitless, so they say things like, "Why bother?"

Take a minute before you go any further and ask yourself which category you fall into. Be honest with yourself. Remember, the first step to getting unstuck is identifying the truth.

Here's what I've learned about having a Growth Mindset:

➢ **You must always be learning.** You are either growing and evolving into a better version of yourself or you are slowly dying. There is no in-between. If I stuck $10,000 under my mattress (which, by the way, there is no money under my mattress - so don't come looking for it), and I left it there for 20 years, it would not be worth the same amount in 20 years. It would be worth LESS. The same principle is true with our minds and our lives - we must be growing and developing or we are slowly dying and losing our most valuable resource - our mind

➢ **Failure is essential.** I know some of you just cringed reading that statement, but it's 100% true. Failure is a part of life, and it can be a powerful tool if you use it to "Fail Forward" (which is a great book by John C Maxwell - you should grab a copy). Failure can be your teacher, your friend, and one of the greatest tools in your toolbox if you grow from it. If you spend your life trying to avoid and fear failure, you will die with dreams in your heart and a long list of regrets. Determine right now that you are going to stop fearing failure and instead embrace it and choose to always learn from it.

> **Feedback is essential.** You must seek out and accept feedback from other people in your life. Feedback helps you learn from mistakes, understand how others see you, and builds your self-confidence. Feedback comes in various forms. It can be feedback from your spouse on how they feel your relationship is going, what they appreciate about you, and what area they'd like to see improvement in. It can be from a boss, clarifying expectations and communicating valuable information about the job you are doing so you can grow to the next level in your career. The biggest place I get feedback in my own life is from my own personal and business coaches. This provides me a safe place to show up and be 100% transparent about things going on in my life and business, get an outside perspective, and learn from someone who has walked similar roads. It is also important that you get feedback from the right people, not just anyone. Let's be real…there are a lot of people in your life who you don't need OR want feedback from. Putting out a post on social media asking for feedback about your new haircut may be okay, but when it comes to going through your hard time and embracing failure, you want to be selective about who you let speak into your life. Not everyone deserves that right.

How To Get It:

1. Constantly be reading, learning, AND trying new things. You won't agree with everything you read, and you won't love every new thing you try, but that's how you grow yourself AND it's also how you gain more self-awareness about yourself.

2. Think about a hard time or failure in your recent past and stop and ask yourself, "What did I learn from that?"

3. You must be intentional about your personal growth. Growth doesn't have to be hard, but it does have to be intentional. You must invest in your own growth with your time, energy, and resources.

You've taken a great step just by reading this book! It won't just automatically happen.

4. Getting proper feedback is essential. In reference to a hard time you are going through, the first thing I would do is ask myself, "Who do I know who has been through something similar and is better from it?" I would also ask myself, "Do I trust and respect this person enough to accept feedback from them?"

Checklist

- ☐ Growth mindset people never give up, embrace challenges, and are constantly learning.
- ☐ Fixed mindset people give up easily, avoid challenges, and feel like it's fruitless to learn - they like to be the "smartest person in the room".
- ☐ You must always be learning and growing or you are dying. There is no middle ground.
- ☐ Make failure your friend and teacher instead of something you spend the rest of your life trying to avoid.
- ☐ Seek out feedback and accept criticism from people you respect.
- ☐ Learn or try something new every day.
- ☐ Don't waste your failures. Always ask yourself, "What can I learn from this failure?"
- ☐ Make an intentional personal growth action plan. Start simple and build on it. A great coach can help you do that as well.

Self-Coaching Questions

✓ Do I embrace challenges or give up easily?
✓ What could you do differently next time?
✓ What is one new thing I've been putting off trying?
✓ If you knew you couldn't fail, what goal would you go for?

CHAPTER 6

EVERYTHING IS HAPPENING FOR YOU, NOT TO YOU

There Is a Bigger Plan at Work

"It's not what happens in life that bothers us. It's what we're believing about it that bothers us." - Byron Katie

After 3 years of full-time travel, constantly staying in new places, sleeping in different beds and figuring out how to function in yet another space week over week, the Hensler family was ready to settle down for a bit and call someplace home! A house came on the market for rent in a city and state we came to know and love, Oriental, NC. So we decided it was time to call this place home and plant some roots…at least for the next year. We went through the process, signed the lease papers, and began our search for furniture. Since we had been renting fully furnished Airbnbs, we owned very little besides the clothes on our backs.

About a week before we were supposed to take possession of that house, some things came to our attention about the owner, the house, and the real estate management company that were concerning us. So we set up a meeting with the property manager to see if we could clear the air. As we sat in her office, I knew with everything inside of me that I needed to hand her back the keys, ask for my security deposit back, and walk away from this deal. So two hours later, with my mascara totally covering my face and some pretty harsh words spoken, we walked out of that office. Everyone's emotions were high as reality set in that we were once again back in limbo, having no idea where we were going to live in two weeks. Quite frankly, the process of constantly figuring it out was exhausting for us. Not to mention all of the emotions flooding my heart of the injustice we just experienced, the lying and the incompetence - all things that hit me at my core. I allowed myself to stay in my pity party for the evening but knew the next day I needed to step out of the emotions and figure out our next steps.

But it wasn't that simple. We had already put some furniture in the garage at what was supposed to be "our new house". So now we had to once again deal with the incompetent property manager to meet her there to get our belongings. We scheduled a time to meet her. In the meantime, a friend at another real estate company began searching for available rentals for us, and they were working hard for us without any guarantee of getting our business. We decided that, before we met the property manager, we would run to Panera and grab some pastries for the real estate company that was helping us out, to show our appreciation. Since we weren't living close to the city, it was a 30-minute drive one way to get to Panera, but we took the drive. On the way back to drop off the bagels and meet the property manager at the house, Matt realized we were going to be a few minutes late, so he thought he better speed up. What he didn't realize was there was a cop radaring. As the sirens blared and I saw the blue lights in the rearview mirror, my heart sank. I felt like someone punched me in the gut. Not because Matt was speeding. Not because we were going to be even later. But because the other thing no one else knew at the time was how badly we were struggling financially. We were barely feeding our family; we had just come off two months of eating rice and beans literally. I knew that an out-of-state speeding ticket was going to cost us at least $500 by the time it was said and done.

Here we were trying to do something good for someone else, giving out of our own need and pain, already under the stress of having no idea where we were going to live in two weeks, and how we were going to feed our family, and now this. I was sick.

Here's the thing, friends. In that moment, it felt like everything was happening to us. It felt like we were the victims of a bad movie. It felt like our world was falling apart, and it was hard to see how it was really falling together. And yes, that ticket cost us upwards of $550 and with a pit in my stomach, I dropped that check off, knowing that was our grocery money and I'd have to figure out another way.

Looking back on that situation, we realized that if our plan went the way we thought it should at the time, we would have been stuck in an area without opportunity and continued to struggle just to get by. But those doors closed for a reason and the right doors opened that landed us in a better situation for the years to follow.

It's so easy to feel like a victim in these types of situations and to feel like the world is against you, but I have learned that even moments like this are happening FOR me, not TO me. Some of you want to slam the book shut right now because you don't want to hear that your hard time is happening for you. You just want it to stop. Friend, I get it. I've been through many of them myself, but I can honestly tell you if you start looking at your hard times and obstacles in your life for what they are offering you, it will free you from sitting in the corner and having a pity party.

Here's what I've learned about filtering hard things through a mindset of them Happening For Me and Not To Me:

> ➢ **You must drop the victim mentality.** The moment you take ownership of your own life, something inside of you shifts. You immediately see things in a different way. Even when it feels like it, you stop believing that the world is against you. You don't ignore the truth or fake positivity as we've already discussed. You state the

truth but you do it through a lens of a growth mindset and owning your own life.

➤ **Nothing is ever wasted, it's stored.** Every single struggle we go through is used to grow us, change us, and help us become the person we were created to be. Even when I told you the story in the chapter on perspective about all the years I spent struggling with my mental health, those were not wasted years. I gained so much through those years, and I learned so much about myself through those years that make me the person I am today. The same is true for you. Whatever you are going through, it will be used to make you better, help someone else, and propel you towards the purpose God put you on this earth to do. I love the lyrics in Nichole Nordeman's song - "Every mile mattered."

➤ **There is a bigger plan at work.** I'll cover this more in Chapter 14 on Prayer, but when you put your trust and faith in Someone bigger than yourself - it makes the process of trusting there is a bigger plan at work a whole lot easier. I believe with every fiber of my being that things happen for a reason and God knows how to shut and open the right doors for me. When I'm going through hard times, it gives me peace and confidence that I couldn't have any other way.

➤ **Express gratitude.** I love this quote by Kristin Armstrong -" When we focus on our gratitude, the tide of disappointment goes out and the tide of love rushes in." Gratitude will help you see all that's going right for you instead of looking at all that's going wrong. Gratitude will help your heart remember all the things you have to be grateful for, even in moments of deep struggle and pain. If gratitude isn't part of your life - make it part of your life. This isn't meant to be a comprehensive book on gratitude - but there are many out there. Go get yourself one and read it if this is an area you need to grow in.

How To Get It:

1. Give yourself parameters on self-pity. Decide right now how long you will give yourself to indulge in self-pity when something bad happens. Don't expect yourself to never fall into self-pity, we all do it. But only allow yourself to stay there for so long. Is it two hours, overnight, a day, two days? What's your parameter? If you need to, tell a friend to hold you accountable the next time you find yourself there.

2. Ask yourself the hard question - "Are there areas of my life that I am waiting on someone else to fix or change that I need to take responsibility for myself?"

3. Shift your mindset. Ask yourself, "How can I view my current hard time through a lens of it happening FOR me instead of TO me?" "How can I learn, grow, and help someone else as a result of this?"

4. Put your trust in a higher power. For me personally, that's God. I honestly don't think I'd be sitting here writing this book if it wasn't for my faith and trust in Him my entire life. Life's hard, and it's even harder when you try to do it alone.

Checklist

- ☐ Drop the victim mentality and take ownership.
- ☐ Set up parameters for yourself around self-pity.
- ☐ Remember, your hard times are never wasted.
- ☐ Trust that there is a bigger plan at work.
- ☐ Cultivate an attitude of gratitude.
- ☐ Ask yourself what areas of your life you need to take responsibility for.
- ☐ Reflect on current and past hard times and how those things worked out for you.

Self-Coaching Questions

- ✓ Where are you irresponsible?
- ✓ How is this affecting you?
- ✓ What are the little things in your life right now that you are grateful for?

CHAPTER 7

OLD STORY

Stop Being Stuck in Your Past

"You can't start the next chapter of your life if you keep re-reading the last one."

- Anonymous

As I started a Zoom coaching call with one of my clients (yes, this story is used with permission - let's call him Dave), he expressed to me how frustrated he was because he couldn't seem to get anywhere in his life and anytime he tried to do something different, nothing worked. His marriage was in turmoil at the moment, he had very little motivation for life, wasn't passionate about his career, and was telling himself that doing the growth to get him beyond it was just going to be too hard. He also expressed to me that he had worked through this all before in counseling and grabbed some tools from that, so he was coping better than he had in the past, but was still stuck and exasperated.

I explained to him that the reason nothing is working is because everything he was trying was still going through the filter of an "old story" he had been telling himself since his childhood. I said, "Let's uncover what that story is and replace it with a new story, and then you will start seeing progress. And by the way, this doesn't have to be months of therapy sessions, nor does it need to be some deep, dark conversation." He was skeptical to say the least and was like, "I don't really see how it's going to be that easy. I have been dealing with this for years, actually decades." His skepticism was fair, but I also knew the power of what I was about to walk him through.

So we dove in and uncovered what the "old story" was he was really telling himself, and where that came from, and then we re-wrote the new story. About 45 minutes later, in that ONE coaching session, his countenance changed, the light bulbs went on, and it all clicked for him. He just kept saying, "I can't believe this was that easy. I'm still not convinced this is going to stick." But I just encouraged him to walk out what we talked about on our call and watch how his life changes.

Over the next several weeks, he did the work and changed his mindset and, bit by bit, began regaining his motivation, his zeal for life, and had a newfound hope that he was actually going to be able to live in his "new story". A few weeks later, his wife looked me in the eyes and said, "Christie, Dave has a spring in his step now and it's all because of what you did with him. He said it truly changed his life, and I can see it, too." I reassured her that it was life-changing, but ultimately, he was the one who did the work. I just guided him through the process. That's the power of effective coaching, friends.

Here's what I've learned about our Old Story:

> **We don't normally even recognize we are living in it.** The first step is realizing that somewhere along the way in our lives, usually early on, we adopt limiting beliefs about ourselves, negative thinking patterns, and things that keep us from reaching our potential. Sometimes these are assumptions we make about ourselves. Sometimes they are things others say to us through their own pain that aren't true, but we adopt them as our truth. These beliefs

become a story we tell ourselves throughout our entire life, and we may not even realize it. For me personally, an old story I told myself for years was, "I'm not worthy of being loved for who I am. I have to earn any kind of love or support I get."

➤ **We all have gifts and gaps from growing up.** I don't honestly remember where I learned this, but it was powerful. During the course of our childhood, we all have gifts and gaps from our upbringing. Gifts are the things our parents or caretakers gave us. Maybe they provided well for our physical needs. Maybe they believed in us and encouraged us. Maybe they gave us a great education. Maybe they modeled a great marriage to you. These are gifts that were given to you and me. On the flip side, there were also gaps for all of us growing up. There were things that our parents or caretakers didn't give us. Usually, these things weren't given to us because the people raising us didn't have the capacity to give them to us, because they didn't possess them themselves. Maybe they grew up with a father who provided for their physical needs but had no capacity to meet their emotional needs because he never had his own emotional needs met and didn't even know how to do that. What happens, though, is we don't view these gaps for what they are - GAPS. We tend to view them as defects in ourselves, like something is inherently wrong with us. We start believing we are messed up, when in fact, we just had gaps in our upbringing that we need to close in other ways now to become the best version of ourselves.

BONUS TIP: Viewing it this way also helps you release resentment towards people in your life for things they didn't have the capacity to give you.

➤ **You don't have to be stuck in your old story.** Sometimes all we need to know is that we don't have to keep living through that old story. Maybe you told yourself you were a disappointment to everyone in your life, all your life. You can stop living in that story NOW. No matter how many years you have lived it, it's not too late to break out of it.

> ➤ **You don't have to go through months of therapy to get out of your old story.** Just because you have been living an old story for years doesn't mean it will take you years to create the new story. It also doesn't mean you have to get deep in the weeds of every bad thing everyone ever said or did to you to walk free from it. Whew! For someone like myself, that was freeing news to know I didn't have to sit in some counseling office for months, with a scratchy Kleenex in my hand and tears streaming down my face, while having to relive every bad thing that happened to me. Nope.

How To Get It:

1. If you are stuck and going around the same mountains, you probably are living through an old story. Be aware of that possibility.

2. Ask yourself, "What beliefs do you have about yourself?" "Where did they come from?" "Who did they come from?"

3. How are these old beliefs showing up in your life? Maybe they are showing up in your marriage and how you interact with your spouse. Maybe they are showing up in the fact that every time you start to pursue your dreams, you quit. Maybe they are showing up in the way you let other people treat you. Take an honest look at areas of your life where you are struggling and ask yourself if those beliefs are found there.

4. Use the reclamation process that is listed in Chapter 1 of Identify The Truth (Is this the truth?) to help you identify what the truth is about the old story you have been telling yourself.

5. Write the new story. Decide what new story you are going to write. For example, when I realized I was living through an old story of "I'm not worthy", which was causing me to not stand up for myself in certain situations or set certain boundaries, I had to decide that I am worthy, and my worth isn't based on what I earn or do, it's based on WHO I am. I also decided that no one gets my power unless I give it away. So that was the new story I started living through.

6. "Spot, Stop, Swap" is an excellent tool to actually walk through this process on a daily basis until your new story becomes the default in your mind and in your life. The video explaining this tool is in the FREE resources section at www.lifehacksforhardtimes.com.

Checklist

☐ Recognize that you may be living in an old story, and that's the reason you keep going around the same mountains and can't break free in certain areas of your life, even the ones you are in counseling for.

☐ Identify what your old story is. What limiting beliefs have you carried with you most of your life?

☐ Acknowledge and be thankful for the gifts in your upbringing.

☐ Acknowledge the gaps in your upbringing for what they were - GAPS, not defects in YOU.

☐ You don't need to go to some deep, dark place and have months of therapy to rewrite your story. And if you decide to go that route, make sure you have someone who knows how to get you beyond it and not keep you in it.

☐ Ask yourself, "Where and who did my old beliefs come from?"

☐ Identify how the old beliefs are showing up in your life at this moment.

☐ Go through the reclamation process to help you break out of it. (Find that in Chapter 1.)

☐ Write your new story.

☐ Use "Spot, Stop, Swap" to keep your mindset in check every day, until your new story becomes the default thought pattern for your life.

☐ Experience freedom and acknowledge it!

Self-Coaching Questions

✓ What's really holding you back?
✓ What limiting beliefs have you carried with you through your life? (In any area - health, relationships, finances, yourself, family, God)
✓ How are these limiting beliefs affecting you?
✓ What's your first step on your new path (story)?

CHAPTER 8

EMBRACE PAIN

Sometimes the Only Way Out Is Through

"People go through so much pain trying to avoid pain." - Neil Strauss

It's 3am and I'm standing in my bedroom with only a t-shirt on, running on pure fumes and already 8 hours into labor when my midwife looks me straight in the eyes and says, "Christie, stay with me; you have to do this and you have to keep your head in it or it's not going to end well."

This was the birth of my third child, so this wasn't my first rodeo, but this one was different for several reasons. I was at the lowest point in my entire life, fighting every day just to survive the grip of panic and anxiety, OCD, fear, feeling totally overwhelmed and burnt out. A few weeks prior to going into labor, I candidly said to Matt, "Can we please put this child up for adoption? I can't even handle the 2 kids I already have and can't even get through a day without someone by my side. I don't see how I'm going to handle another child." In his non-emotional, objective way that he always has, he kindly responded, "No. We are going to figure it out and get through this." I believed him, but I was running out of fight.

That Friday evening when my body went into labor, I was already physically exhausted and ready to sleep for the night. The labor was the hardest of the three. I had people throughout my house everywhere - a friend, my mom, a photographer, 2 midwives, and Matt. The threat of going to the hospital for a c-section loomed over my head and was the last place I wanted to find myself. My mental state was not good and was part of the reason this labor was the hardest thus far. I sat on my bed having no idea what I was going to do and glanced over at a small framed print on my nightstand that read, "Be still and know that I am God." All I had the energy to mutter to Him that night was "I trust you."

A transformer went out that night on our road and we lost power for the night. Thankfully, we had a generator. I guarantee you, we were the only house on the street that night with 8 cars in the driveway, all the lights on, and a garden hose running out the top balcony to the sewer drain to empty the water from the birthing tub.

This child was refusing to come out! We tried everything from getting in the bathtub to nipple stimulation, to an exercise ball, but it just kept dragging out! Every minute felt like an hour. And every contraction felt like the last one I could handle. I held on with every ounce of my being that night in pure pain in every way, shape, and form. I reached within and pulled out grit I didn't know I had. But at 8:30am the next morning, Madeline Jane was born. She is full of spunk, loves life, and I honestly couldn't imagine life without her.

PAIN. That's a four-letter word to most of us. Whether it's physical, mental or emotional pain, it's something we try to avoid, numb, or run from. But I want to show you in this chapter how embracing pain can actually serve you well as you go through hard times and endeavor to live your best life.

First a caution. There are situations in our lives where there are types of pain we need to embrace and walk through. However, there are also situations in our lives that are types of pain we need to not tolerate and set very firm boundaries. When I say embrace pain in this chapter, I am referring to the types of pain you need to work through, like improving your marriage, working out frustrations with your boss, digging deep, and figuring out why the rejection you experienced from a friend hurt so bad, and so on. I am NOT suggesting that you endure or embrace pain from an abusive relationship, someone manipulating or taking advantage of you in any way, shape or form, or any kind of self-harm.

Now that that is clear. **Here's what I've learned about Embracing Pain in my own life:**

> **First, differentiate between something toxic and something that just needs course corrected.** You must first be able to confidently know that the pain you are walking through is necessary. The relationship that you need to fix is worth it and you need to dive in and course correct it, even though it is painful. If you are in a toxic situation, then you need to stop embracing pain and get out. Don't skip this step. In my story above, that was clearly a moment where I needed to embrace the pain and walk through it. You'll read many more stories in this book where you will see I had to make the decision and embrace the pain through it.

> **Determine to grow through it, not just go through it.** It's important to decide that whatever pain you are going through, you are going to adopt a growth mindset and learn and grow from it. The last thing you want to do is just endure a whole bunch of pain and not learn anything from it, and then go repeat the process through something else. I saw this quote somewhere, "Pain can be a gift if you are willing to find its meaning behind the mess."

> **Allow yourself to feel all the feelings.** Sometimes when you are dealing with something, it can feel like walking across broken glass, but it's important that you allow yourself to FEEL what you are feeling. Don't try to lie to yourself about how you are really feeling. Remember our very first step: identify the truth. I'll dive more into Emotions in Chapter 18 so you'll have the tools to do this.

> ➤ **Do not try to distract, escape, or numb the pain.** All that does is put off the healing process even longer. I remember when I was recovering from that hot mess of a relationship, I shared with you in Chapter 1, the feelings I felt were so awful. All I wanted was for them all to go away and feel peace and joy. All I wanted to do was bury those feelings in another relationship or distract myself by starting two businesses, but it wasn't until I actually allowed myself to feel all the feelings without numbing them that I was truly able to heal and reach a place of closure and wholeness.

How To Get It:

1. Determine if the pain is toxic or something you need to embrace. If you are hesitant in any way, I would encourage you to get feedback from someone you know and trust about your situation.

2. Decide if you are going to walk through it or walk away from it. Based on your determination in Step 1, make a decision and then stick with it. Don't waiver in limbo.

3. Allow yourself to feel the feelings. Don't criticize or judge yourself for the feelings you are feeling. Write them down on paper, get them out, and allow yourself to feel them.

4. Ask yourself, "What are these feelings telling me?" More on this in Chapter 18. For example, if you are feeling angry - ask yourself what's behind that anger.

5. Use this opportunity to gain self-awareness about yourself and how you handle pain. This is a great time to identify things about yourself that you may not see clearly when times are peaceful and easy.

6. Take intentional and positive action in whichever direction you decide to go. Do not sit in it. If you decide to grow through it, then start walking through it on purpose. If you decide to walk away, then start moving.

Checklist

- [ ] Determine if this is a pain you need to walk through or walk away from.
- [ ] Set your mind to grow through it and learn from it, rather than just endure it.
- [ ] Allow yourself to feel the feelings without judging them or being hard on yourself.
- [ ] Ask yourself questions about the feelings to increase your self-awareness.
- [ ] Don't distract, numb, or escape the pain.
- [ ] Take intentional, positive action with the choice you made.
- [ ] Get support in the situation if you need it. More on that in Chapter 25.

Self-Coaching Questions

- ✓ What do you need to know in order to move forward?
- ✓ What are you most afraid of?
- ✓ What would you say to a friend?
- ✓ What does your heart tell you?

CHAPTER 9

KNOW YOUR PURPOSE

Why Am I Here? And Where Am I Going?

"Without vision, you have no direction. Without direction, you have no purpose."

- Steve Gilliland

As I lay on my bedroom floor shaking in sheer terror and panic, desperately begging God to take me and contemplating taking my own life, I clearly saw a vision. I was standing on a stage in front of a sea of people, offering them hope and a way out of their own mess. Right there on my bedroom floor, in the middle of a full-fledged panic attack, I knew with every fiber of my being that I must continue fighting and overcoming the battle I was in. I knew if I could get to the other side, I would have the tools to equip and inspire others to get to the other side of their own battle…no matter how hopeless they felt.

I wish I could tell you that the next day I was walking in freedom and living my purpose, but instead, it took me years to continue to fight for freedom in my life. Then, once I turned a corner and began my path to freedom, it took me several more years to reset my mind, overcome fears, and live free from the bondage of panic, anxiety, OCD and irrational fears.

When I look back on those years and how tormenting they were, I started asking myself what made me keep fighting? What gave me the grit and resilience to keep pushing day after day through living hell to the other side? Some would think it was my amazing husband. Some would think it was my cute kids. Others would think it was an interior-designed house. It was none of those things. It was that vision I saw that day lying on the hardwood floor of my bedroom, begging God to not let me wake up the next day.

Why am I telling you this story? It's surely not because I like reliving it, but it is because it shows the incredible power of having purpose and vision in our lives. It is so powerful that even when I wanted my life to end, it kept me going because I saw a better future through the pain, I was living in.

Here's what I've learned about Purpose and Vision:

➢ **You must clearly define it in your life.** Your purpose is "why you are here". Your vision is "where you are going". Without knowing why you wake up every day, life gets mundane, boring, and when it's hard, you wonder if it's even worth it. If you know why you are here but have no idea where you are going, then it's impossible to know if you've arrived. You spend your time wandering aimlessly through each day, like a boat without rudders.

➢ **It gives you something to focus on while you are working through your hard time.** When you are standing in a pile of horse manure, and all you do is look down at your boots while smelling the awful stench, you can only tolerate and endure that for so long. But even when you are standing in the manure, if you can look up and look ahead at a brighter future, it gives you the perseverance and the tenacity to keep moving through your mess because you know the manure you are standing in is only for a season. It allows you to

54

handle that hard time with much more grace and contentment because you know you aren't staying there, and you know exactly where you are headed.

- ➤ **Purpose fuels you to keep going.** Passion linked with purpose becomes the fuel to keep going even when you aren't sure how things are going to come together. It gives you perseverance when things are difficult.

- ➤ **Purpose and Vision act as a compass.** Being clear on your purpose and vision allows you to easily identify your priorities and make decisions (more on Decision Making in Chapter 20). You have to know why you are doing the things you are doing, and purpose answers that question for you.

How To Get It:

1. One question Coach Valorie Burton uses to help her clients identify their purpose is, "How are people's lives better when they cross my path?" In other words, what do you have to offer the world?

2. Another way to identify your purpose is to know your strengths and your passions. When you can identify the things you are great at (your strengths) and the things you are passionate about, you can usually find your purpose there.

3. To identify your vision, ask yourself, "Where am I headed?" "What does my life look like when I get there?" "What does the person running my business look and act like?" "What does my marriage look like when I arrive at my vision of what I want it to be?" You can determine a vision for your life as a whole or you can determine visions for specific areas of your life. One way I like to do that is with the Life Wheel.

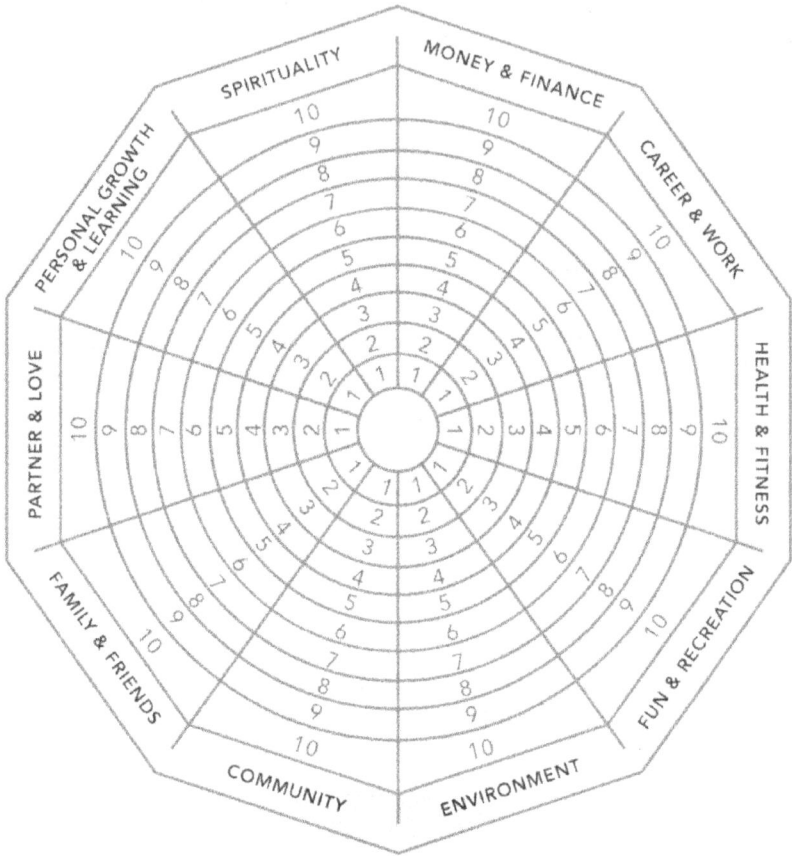

Life Wheel

For detailed instructions on using the Life Wheel, download the free resources for this book at www.lifehacksforhardtimes.com.

Checklist

- ☐ You must clearly define your purpose and vision.

- ☐ Knowing your purpose and vision will enable you to be content in the hard season you are in, while working towards something better. It will keep you forward-focused, even while standing in the manure.

- ☐ Knowing your purpose will give you perseverance to keep going, even when you can't see how it all will work out.

- ☐ Purpose and vision act as a compass to help you identify your priorities and make better decisions.

- ☐ Identify your purpose and vision by answering the questions above in this chapter as well as the ones in the self-coaching section.

- ☐ Identify your strengths and passions and look for your purpose where those two intersect each other.

For more specific coaching to help you identify your purpose and vision, check out my latest workshops and group-coaching bundles at www.lifehacksforhardtimes.com.

Self-Coaching Questions

✓ How are people's lives better when they cross my path?
✓ What are my top 5 strengths?
✓ What am I passionate about?
✓ Where am I headed in my life in 1 year, 2 years, 5 years?
✓ What does my ideal scenario look like?

CHAPTER 10

SEASONS

This Too Shall Pass

"No winter lasts forever; no spring skips its turn." - Hal Borland

O n February 1st, 2016, my family and I pulled out of my parents' driveway in a 1994 Fleetwood Bounder motorhome. We had just closed on the sale of our house and gave away and sold just about everything we owned. We were about to embark into uncharted territory on an adventure we had planned to last 6 to 12 months. Little did we know that adventure would end up lasting years.

Before we even arrived at our first destination, we found ourselves with a broken windshield and driving through a tornado, which took out our generator. Then, in the months that followed, we were stranded with a bad starter in the middle of Louisiana at 10pm. We were stranded in the countryside of Kentucky on Mother's Day with a tire blowout. We lost our brakes traveling the hills of San Antonio and found ourselves broken down along the 8-lane highway outside of Dallas with no transmission at 10pm. We hit a closet organizer on the highway outside of Indianapolis and busted our (new) transmission lines. We had rocks stuck in our rotors, which left us on the side of the road in Branson, Missouri. We had a leaking anti-freeze tank in the middle of Houston, TX. We were incredibly thankful for Good Sam towing coverage. There is more, but you get the point.

On the flip side, we met some amazing people, made new friends, and re-kindled old friendships. We experienced memories we would never have had, and learned an incredible amount of resourcefulness and adaptability. We learned to laugh instead of cry, dance in the rain, and make memories through the horse manure. I remember when we were sitting in the Louisiana gas station that night, knowing that we had to get a repair guy out there to replace the starter, and Nevaeh looked at us and said, "Who thought this was a good idea to sell our house and do this?" Matt and I looked at each other and laughed. Then, in the pouring rain, we ran inside the gas station to kindly let the clerk know that our RV was broken down and wouldn't start, so we'd be sitting here for a bit, but a repair tech was on the way. To which she responded, "Thank you for letting me know, but can you please move your RV because it is blocking the pumps?" I'll let you fill in the blanks on that one.

Life on the road was exhilarating and exhausting at the same time. We had the constant pressure of figuring out where to go next, managing repairs, and learning new cities. But we had the constant thrill of seeing new people every week, exploring new cities, and wondering what was going to happen next!

Even when we wanted this life-on-the-road season to be over, we would run into closed doors, like my previous story about the house in NC, that continually kept us "on the road". But instead of crying in a corner or waiting to be happy until we got what we wanted to be happy, we decided to make the most of it, knowing this was a season in our life, and it wouldn't last forever.

Here's what I've learned about Seasons:

➢ **Balance is a myth.** So many times we try to find balance in our lives, and we think we'll be peaceful and secure when everything is perfectly balanced. We will spend just the right amount of time with our children, we'll have a certain number of scheduled date nights with our spouse, we'll work X number of hours a week, make sure we get 8 hours of sleep at night, drink our 64 ounces of water a day, pray and meditate. We'll do community service and have our checkbook completely balanced once a week. If you are accomplishing all of that consistently, then you should go write a book on it. But in my experience, balance is a myth, and striving for balance leads to continual frustration and feelings of defeat. I prefer to look at life as seasons. There are seasons where you need to be more present with your children. There are seasons where you may have to work long hours to get a business off the ground so you have the time freedom you are striving for in the future. There are seasons of pain, and there are seasons of joy. There are seasons of sickness, and there are seasons of health. When you can stop trying to balance everything and start recognizing the season you are in and what priorities you should have in that season, it keeps life simple…as it should be.

➤ **Seasons always pass.** The other thing I have realized is whether your season is amazing or awful - it's going to pass. Just like the seasons of the Earth change, the seasons of our life change. If you are in a great season of life, soak it all in, be present in the moment, and be thankful for all that is in it. If you are in a hard season of life, be encouraged that it won't last, it will pass, and choose to grow through it.

➤ **How to be content, not complacent, while moving towards something better.** Another myth people believe is if they decide to be content in their current season of life, that means they are settling for what is. I have found that you can be content without being complacent, and the key to that is having a purpose and vision that you are always moving towards (more on that in Chapter 9). You can learn to grow where you are planted, find joy in the journey, and be content WHILE anticipating and moving towards something. It's more than possible; I've done it for the last 20 years of my life. Let me show you how.

How To Get It:

1. Recognize the season you are in and everything that goes with it. Remember, identify the truth of your situation (are you seeing a pattern here?).

2. Understand what your top 1-3 priorities need to be in this season. Acknowledge how long this season should last (if you know, you may not). Remove any distractions or clutter in your life that are taking your attention away from your priorities for this season. For example, if you are trying to build a business (which is hard!) during that season, you don't have the capacity to volunteer for 3 different organizations, sing in the church choir, drive your kids to 7 extra-curricular activities a week, and remodel your master bathroom. You cannot do it all.

3. Have a vision that you are always moving toward. This is imperative, and I went over this in complete detail in Chapter 9.

4. Figure out how to grow where you are planted. You must learn to make the most of your season while you are moving towards something better. Let me give you a simple example. As I've experienced life on the road and am still waiting for my final, forever home, I decided that I must not live temporarily, and I needed to enjoy my space, so I found a love and passion for houseplants. They bring me so much enjoyment, they purify the air, and they are mine.

5. Find beauty in the simple things. There is beauty and enjoyment all around us. Is it the handmade pottery mug you are drinking your coffee from? Is it the blanket you have on your lap while reading this book? Is it the classy phone case you have on your phone that makes you smile? Is it the birds in your bird feeder? (More on this in Find Joy in the Journey Chapter 16.)

Checklist

☐ Balance is a myth. Stop chasing it and understand the season you are in.

☐ No matter how hard the season, remember, it will pass.

☐ Be content in your current season while having a bigger vision you are moving towards.

☐ Stop and recognize the season you are in and determine your top 1-3 priorities in this season.

☐ Know your purpose and vision and take daily action towards it. (Chapter 9)

☐ Figure out ways to grow where you are planted right now.

☐ Find beauty in the simple things all around you. (Chapter 16)

Self-Coaching Questions

✓ What is life teaching you right now?
✓ What do you want to be different in your life one year from now?
✓ If you look back a few years from now, what will you wish you would
✓ have done in this current season?
✓ How do you want to show up in this season?

CHAPTER 11

MASTER YOUR SUBCONSCIOUS

Controlling Your Lizard Brain

"The single most powerful asset we have is our mind. If trained well, it can create enormous wealth." - Robert Kiyosaki

In the first chapter, I mentioned being put in the mental health ward after a relationship ended. I'm going to continue that story now to show you how knowing how to "master my subconscious" helped set me free in that situation.

As I lay in the hospital bed, I had calmed down from my emotional breakdown earlier that night. At this point, a couple of my best friends were by my side, I had some chocolate, and I was thinking clearly. I was emotionally spent, but my head was back on straight. It was about 3am, so the hospital staff gave me a proposal. They said, "You can either go home now and come back next week to the hospital for counseling OR you can switch rooms for the night and go home in the morning." Well, the last thing I was going to do next week was to come back to the hospital for counseling.

So, since it was 3am, it made sense for me to just tough it out a few more hours and go home and move on with my life. However, I wasn't expecting what was about to happen next. They then packed up my stuff and moved me…in a van…to the mental health ward…without telling me. They walked me into that place, shut the metal doors behind me, and immediately took everything from me, including the drawstring from my pants and the shoelaces from my shoes. In that moment, intense fear and intense fight rose up within me, and I knew the game was on and I had to win it.

My two biggest fears in life are being controlled and being taken advantage of, and both of those things were happening to me in full force. As my fight or flight responses were on red alert, my mind swirled with options. As I looked around at drugged-up residents, people who couldn't even finish their sentences, and some of them walking around with half their clothes on, I knew I wanted out of there and wanted out of there quick. Was I emotional that evening? Yes! But I wasn't crazy, and I wasn't all drugged up. I didn't belong there.

However, as much as I wanted out of there, I even put my MacGyver skills on and searched to see if I could crawl out the ductwork or window (seriously). I also knew that if I "acted out", that would only give them more reason to keep me there. So, at this moment in time, I had to master every bit of fear, worry, and panic I was feeling, and I had to have my head on. The first thing I did was call my parents. My mom and 74-year-old grandma drove straight from Pittsburgh to St. Louis. I called my friends, and they showed up at the hospital. I called my attorney. I called someone who had worked in these types of facilities. And I had to call my work and tell them I wouldn't be there that day. How do you explain that one? The hospital wouldn't let any of my advocates in to see me. As I stood in the hallways or on the phone, the nursing staff would walk by and taunt me. They would say things like, "You're not getting out of here anytime soon. It's Friday, and there is no way a doctor is coming in here to see you on a Friday night." And I would look them square in the eye, with a very put-together and firm voice, and say, "I will be out of this place by this evening…just watch."

It was December, and they were putting up a Christmas tree, so I decided to join the staff and decorate the tree. They were going to show a movie to the residents, so I popped them all popcorn and served them. They had meetings every hour or two, where they would talk about things like anger management and who knows what else, so I would attend those meetings, nod my head, smile, and participate. I would listen to their psychobabble and just smile. I did this all day long while praying and while telling my subconscious brain to stand firm and calm down.

At 10:30pm that FRIDAY EVENING, a Pakistani doctor walked into that mental ward to see one patient...and it was me. I just so happened to have been in his country in the past doing missionary work, so I immediately connected with him on that level and just started talking to him like he was an old friend I was meeting for coffee. After about 10 minutes, he looked at me and said, "Do you want to stay in here?" I had to withhold yelling, "HECK NO!!!!" But I did very confidently tell him, "No, I don't want to be in here. I had a very bad relationship breakdown, and I was upset, but I don't need to be in a place like this, I just need to work through my broken heart." He looked at me and said, "I'm going to give you my business card so you can make an appointment and come to my office to meet with me." I nodded and smiled. And he said the words I had been longing to hear all day long, "I'm going to release you!" I profusely thanked him and called my friends and said, "Come pick me up!" By this time, it was pushing 11:30pm. And the staff that had taunted me all day was gone, much to my dismay, because I had a few words for them. The rest of the staff gave me back my belongings and I walked out of those doors feeling like I was just set free from 40 years in prison. I jumped in my friends' car and they said, "Do you care if we go to McDonald's?" (They knew I didn't eat at McDonald's). I said, "Go wherever you want - I am FREE!"

Friends, if I wasn't able to master my subconscious that day and control the flood of emotions that filled my heart and mind, I wouldn't have been able to get out of that situation as quickly or as easily as I did.

Here's what I've learned about Mastering Your Subconscious:

➢ **Control your lizard brain.** Robert Kiyosaki, author of Rich Dad Poor Dad (a phenomenal book by the way), explained this concept so well. As you see on the diagram, the comparison of your conscious part of the brain to the subconscious part is dramatic. Some people are considered left-brain people, who tend to be logical, focused on facts, orderly, math and science-minded, and they generally live in realism. Then you have the right-brain people, who are more emotional, focused on art and creativity, occasionally absent-minded, and their imagination predominates their mind. But whether you are more left-brained or right-brained, the majority of your brain is your subconscious mind. This is what Robert likes to refer to as your "lizard brain". Its main purpose is for your survival. It is also your instinctive response to stress and pressure - your fight-or-flight response. This is where fear and worry live. In a primitive world, it keeps you alive. When you sense danger, it tells you either you need to fight this off or run away so you can survive. It gives you a healthy sense of fear in that instance. But in our civilized world, that sometimes acts as a detriment because most things aren't life or death. Therefore, you need to be able to silence that instinct of "Fight! or Run!" so that you can see the challenge before you for what it really is, and you aren't immediately operating out of fear and worry. When you are panicking, you get tunnel vision and can't see things clearly or make wise decisions, because in your fear and panic, it's all about, "How can I escape this situation?!" instead of, "How can I embrace this challenge and grow through it?", like we talked about in Growth Mindset Chapter 5. In the middle of a hard time, it's about staying grounded, seeing all your options, and being able to look for the opportunities.

➢ **"Fear is a reaction, courage is a choice."** Your subconscious mind will immediately react out of fear and worry (because that is what it was designed to do) if you don't master it and consciously choose courage.

➢ **Take fear and emotions out of your decision-making.** When you and I react instead of respond and make decisions based on fear and emotions, that doesn't usually end well. When you are in the middle of a hard time, and emotions like fear and worry are even more elevated, it's imperative that you learn to master those emotions. Remember the old saying, "Worry is like sitting in a rocking chair; it gives you something to do, but gets you nowhere." More on both of these topics in Decision Making Chapter 20 and Emotions Chapter 18.

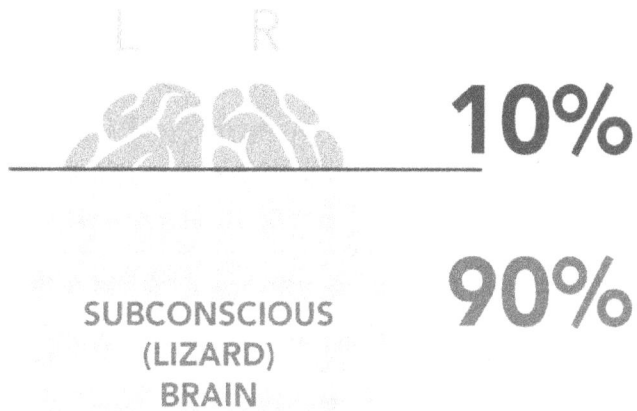

10%

90%

SUBCONSCIOUS
(LIZARD)
BRAIN

How To Get It:

1. The first step is being aware of it. Start recognizing situations when your lizard brain is kicking in and how you are responding to it. Are you being dictated by fear and worry or are you standing up, staying grounded, and making decisions out of courage?

2. Reflect on past decisions you have made based on fear and ask yourself, "How'd that go?"

3. Reflect on past decisions you made, where you left your comfort zone and had courage, and ask yourself, "How'd that go?"

4. Whatever hard time you are currently in, decide that you are going to make confident and courageous decisions, and be intentional about silencing the fear, worry, and red alerts going off in your head.

Checklist

☐ The conscious part of your brain is very small compared to your subconscious brain.

☐ Your subconscious brain, or lizard brain, was meant for your survival. It's your fight-or-flight response. It's necessary to keep you alive.

☐ Recognize that most situations you are facing are not life or death, so you need to be proactive about mastering your subconscious brain.

☐ Mastering your subconscious brain will help you overcome hard things and win at life.

☐ "Fear is a reaction, courage is a choice."

☐ Don't make decisions based on fear and worry.

☐ Reflect on past situations where you reacted in fear and the ones you responded with courage and how things went for you.

☐ Use your past experiences as building blocks to start making decisions with confidence and courage without letting your lizard brain dictate your responses.

Self-Coaching Questions

✓ What are you afraid will happen if you do what you really want to do?

✓ What is causing me to panic about this situation?

✓ What decision am I facing right now where I can choose courage over fear?

✓ What do I need to feel empowered to make this decision?

CHAPTER 12

GRIT

Let's Do This

"Grit is sticking with your future, day in and day out, and not just for the week, not just for the month, but years." - Angela Duckworth

Y ou've already read about the several-year battle I had to overcome panic, anxiety, OCD, irrational fears, and suicidal thoughts. I've already told you how having a vision kept me going in some of the hardest times of my life. The parts of my story I don't always tell are why I never went on medication in the midst of my battle. Or the part about how I couldn't be alone for years, was afraid of every single thing in my house, threw away a lot of stuff I had spent lots of money on over the years, like expensive jewelry and smartphones. Learning how to go to the bathroom by myself was one of the hardest things I have ever done in my life. Not because I forgot "how to go to the bathroom", but because of the terrifying fears and panic that would race through my body at even the thought of doing that by myself. How I learned to travel for years without being able to use the bathroom myself. I knew where every family restroom was on this side of the Mississippi so Matt could go with me. All of the fears I've had to overcome that no one has any idea about. All the things I used to take for granted to be normal, I've had to fight with every ounce of my being to regain normalcy in my life.

So, why am I telling you all of these crazy things at the risk you will decide I am crazy and you stop reading? Well, at this point, I would hope you already made a decision about me and have decided whether I'm someone worth listening to, or you have better things to do with your time.

I'm telling you all of this to prove my point on the power of pure grit in your own life, through your own struggles. You see, sometimes Grit and Resilience are used interchangeably, but they aren't the same thing. In my non-Webster's dictionary definition, resilience is your capacity to weather the storm, stay in the game when it's hard, and not crumble in the middle of the fight. That's important. But in my opinion, you can still come out on the other side of a storm and have resilience, yet be bitter, resentful, and hard. But you fought.

Grit, on the other hand, is the extra effort you put into going through a hard time, because you are determined to grow through it, get something out of it, and leverage the hard times to give you a favorable outcome on the other side, all the while pushing towards your purpose and vision for your life. You're not in it just to make it out of the fight alive; you are in it to make the fight work for you and move you to the next level to reach your God-given purpose and potential. Now for the dictionary definition of grit, "The capacity of a person to maintain their core purpose and integrity in the face of dramatically changed circumstances. The ability to not only overcome setbacks but to also move forward." Do you see the difference between grit and resilience?

So, I've chosen to put Grit in this chapter, because I've seen how having grit in my own life has made me better and moved me closer toward my vision, instead of just being hard and tough.

Here's what I've learned about Grit:

➤ **Growth mindset is fundamental to having grit.** You cannot have grit AND a fixed mindset. People with grit are looking to grow, learn and be better on the other side of their challenges and obstacles…not just endure them. They adopt the "things are happening for me, not to me" mindset, gain perspective, and look for opportunities in the challenges.

➤ **Knowing your purpose and vision is key.** When you know where you are headed and why you are headed there, it is a lot easier to have grit in the midst of your storm because you have something you are moving towards, day in and day out, even when you are standing in the manure.

➤ **Nothing good in life comes easy.** Without grit, it's too easy to give up, throw in the towel, and settle for a less-than-favorable outcome. How you respond to your knockdowns will determine your success in life and in relationships. Anything worth having is not easy, and grit allows you to stay focused and persevere through the hard times.

To dive deeper into this topic, check out Angela Duckworth's book - *Grit: The Power of Passion and Perseverance.*

How To Get It:

1. The first thing you must do is have a growth mindset. If that is still a struggle for you, go back and work through that chapter again (Chapter 5).

2. Define your purpose and vision for your life. This is a key for so many things in your life, and having grit is one of them. *For coaching in this specific area, check out my latest workshops and group-coaching bundles at www.lifehacksforhardtimes.com.

3. Make investing in your own personal growth a priority in your life. Try new things. Gain self-awareness. Get out of your comfort zone. Hire a life coach (who can get you results).

4. Don't give up so easily. Life is messy and pain is part of it. Choose to use your pain and struggles to propel you forward toward your vision and purpose instead of letting it define and defeat you.

Checklist

☐ Grit and resilience are not the same thing. Aim to have both in your life, but grit will help you take your resilience to the next level.

☐ Having a growth mindset is fundamental to having grit.

☐ Knowing your purpose and vision will help you press forward through hard times. If you don't have this defined in your life - make it a priority.

☐ Nothing good in life comes easy. Don't give up. Choose to let your struggles propel you forward.

☐ Invest in your own personal growth. Make it a priority in your life.

☐ Never give up!

Self-Coaching Questions

✓ Do my hard times make me bitter or better?
✓ Am I focused on just getting through my hard times or growing through them?
✓ How can I use my current hard time to move toward my purpose and vision?

DO

E verything you've read in this book so far will only help you overcome the obstacles you are facing IF you put it into action. This section contains a handful of my favorite practical tools I use in my own life and with my clients.

"Hoping drains your energy. Action creates energy." -Robert Kiyosaki

CHAPTER 13

FIND OPPORTUNITY IN THE CHALLENGE

Turning Lemons Into Lemonade

"In the middle of a difficulty lies opportunity." - Albert Einstein

In November of 2015, Matt and I made the grueling and gut-wrenching decision for him to quit his dream engineering job because I was so sick. We decided to take out a home equity loan to provide for our family for a few months. On the same day, he walked out of his office for the last time, walked into the bank to deposit the check from our loan, and we walked away from every bit of financial stability and security we knew. He came home to help me fight a battle I was losing with my mental and physical health. We planned on living on our home equity loan as long as we could, while we continued to fight for answers.

In February of 2016, my answer came to me in a form that I was not expecting - a direct sales company. You just never know where your miracle is going to come from, friends. Now, let me be clear - I was pretty much anti-direct sales. There are some companies with great products, but I didn't love the business model, and there wasn't any way I was going to let my friends have parties in my house or invite my friends over to be pressured into buying something. So that was my stance on direct sales. Now, before those of you in direct sales start sending me nastygrams, finish reading the story.

When I received the email offering me a product that could potentially change my health in such a dramatic way that I could regain my life, I was more than open-minded. After 7 years and over $20k in bills trying all sorts of things, the last thing I was going to do was turn away something that MAY be the answer.

To make an incredibly long story short, against our own beliefs about direct sales, and the fact that what could be the answer we had been searching for for years came in a form we weren't expecting, we took the plunge and joined a direct sales company. I was expecting results, but I wasn't fully expecting what happened next.

The products completely changed my life, so much so that over 6 years later, I don't miss a day without these supplements. For the first time in years, I started sleeping, started being able to finish a sentence, and started feeling normal again. To say I was grateful is an understatement.

However, I also knew that as much as these products were impacting my life and helping me regain my mental and physical health, I still had a long road ahead of me when it came to regaining normalcy in my life. I had built so many twisted mindsets and habits throughout the years that I would have to undo. I knew this wasn't going to be a 3-month process. One of those habits was that I was terrified to be alone; someone was with me every second of the day, yes, even when I had to go to the bathroom or shower. I was NEVER alone...for years. I knew this wasn't something I was just going to walk out of in 2 months' time, which meant the option for Matt to just go get another job was pretty much not possible at the moment, as I was still very much dependent on him.

So we began exploring our options and began looking for opportunities, and here was one right in front of our face. We were part of a direct sales company that we were able to join at a very minimal cost (remember, we were living on credit with no income), and we knew we had life-changing products in our hands. So we decided to build a business with a company and products we believed in, while we rebuilt our life. For a solid 3 years, we built a business that enabled us to work virtually from anywhere, and it also enabled me to start walking out of my mess and rebuilding my life. We were never expecting that one email to change our lives in so many ways.

And no, this isn't a pitch for or against direct sales, but a powerful story of how challenges can provide us tremendous opportunities for growth if we will simply embrace them and look for the opportunities. It's all in our mindset and perspective.

Here's what I've learned about Finding Opportunity in the Challenges:

➢ **You must look at challenges as opportunities, not barriers.** The minute you look at a challenge as a closed door or a brick wall, you immediately lose and fall into a fixed mindset. But, if you can look at your challenge as an opportunity, it will open up a world of options for you.

➢ **Choose to grow through what you go through.** If you will choose to grow through what you are going through, you'll gain lessons that you can carry with you the rest of your life. Those challenges will help you develop into the best version of yourself. A version that will reach potential you didn't even know you had.

➢ **Sometimes closed doors are there for a reason.** I have learned that sometimes the challenges I face and closed doors are meant to course correct me and put me on a different path that is going to lead to where I'm meant to go. It's important that we don't kick down closed doors, but instead, we look for the open windows and other opportunities that are in front of us without trying to control the outcome.

➢ **You can gain tools to equip you for what's ahead.** When you go through challenges and have to build resiliency and do things you weren't planning on doing, learn things you weren't planning on learning, or go through something you'd rather not, those hard times equip and empower you for future hard times so you don't have to learn the same lesson again, assuming you learn it the first time.

How To Get It:

1. The first thing you need to do is shift your mindset. Start viewing challenges as opportunities for growth instead of barriers and annoyances in your life.

2. Proactively look for the opportunities waiting for you in the challenge.

3. Grab the tools you've already learned in this book and put them to work. Perspective, options, gratitude, and growth mindset.

4. Reflect back on the other side of the challenge and realize what you gained as a result of it. When I look back on our experience in direct sales - it gave us life-changing products and a business opportunity when we had nothing to fall back on. But what it also gave me on the other side of it was a ton of self-awareness and personal growth that I have been able to carry forward in my business and with all my coaching clients now. It was an education that I couldn't have paid to get anywhere else.

Checklist

- ☐ Look at challenges as opportunities, not barriers.
- ☐ Choose to grow through what you are going through and develop into a better version of yourself.
- ☐ Sometimes closed doors are there for a reason. Remember, everything is happening for you, not to you.
- ☐ Gain tools from your challenges to equip you for what's ahead in your life.
- ☐ You must shift your mindset or challenges will continue to frustrate you.
- ☐ Be proactive about looking for the opportunities in the challenge.
- ☐ Grab the tools you've already learned in this book and put them to work.
- ☐ Stop and reflect back on the other side of a challenge and realize what you've gained and how you've grown as a person as a result of the challenge.

Self-Coaching Questions

- ✓ What opportunity does this challenge present?
- ✓ What message is being offered in this situation?
- ✓ What tools did I gain by going through this?

CHAPTER 14

PRAYER

Pray Through It

"Prayer should always be our first response to every situation." - Joyce Meyer

I'll never forget the day I was scrubbing down walls at the local Dairy Queen where I was working, and my boss said, "Christie, your dad is on the phone and wants to talk to you." My heart sank because I had a feeling I knew what this call was about. I went and picked up the phone, and on the other end, I heard my dad's voice, "Mark isn't doing well; he's in the ICU at the hospital and they're running some tests."

I was 17 at the time, and Mark was one of my best friends. He was also supposed to be my prom date in a couple of months. He loved Jesus and people, but he had been fighting a battle with leukemia, and it appeared he was starting to lose that battle.

I finished up my work, went home, and changed. In the midst of it all, I just cried out to God and sang some worship songs in my head. Then I headed to Pittsburgh with one of our pastors to see my dear friend. By the time I got there, he had numerous wires hooked up to his brain, as they were monitoring him to see if he was brain dead. A couple of hours later, I watched the screen as his brain waves, which should be going up and down, were just making a straight line across the screen, and I knew what the outcome would be.

That night, I lost one of my best friends. That was the first real loss I had suffered at that point in my young life. That was one of my first crossroads where I had to decide if I believed the God I prayed to answered prayer or not. I chose to believe that day that His ways aren't always our ways. And throughout the years of my life that followed, I would have many opportunities to understand that God always answers prayers; it's just not always in the way I expect Him to answer them.

Now, whether you believe in prayer or a higher power or not, is your choice. And while it's not the focus of this book, it has been a tool in my toolbox that I have used for decades and won't be without.

Here's what I've learned about Prayer:

➢ **God always answers prayer, just not always in the way you expect Him to.** At first, it's easy to question why God isn't delivering you from your hard situation or why He lets bad things happen to good people. But my experience in my own life has been that God opens and shuts the doors that need to be opened and shut according to His plan for my life. I don't always see the whole picture, He does. I don't always know what's best for me, He does. I don't always know what the future holds, He does. I've learned that His timing and His answers are perfect. And I filter His answers and His timing through a lens of a growth mindset as we talked about earlier in the book, so I'm embracing the challenges and growing through the hard times.

➢ **Prayer is communicating and being dependent on a power higher than yourself.** There is a relief and a peace that comes with knowing the world isn't on my shoulders, especially through hard times. When I'm struggling with something, I'm already under extra stress and pressure, and to know I have Someone ready and willing to communicate with me, and with whom I can cast my cares upon, brings me great comfort in my times of need.

➢ **You have to have confidence in your higher power.** You must believe that the higher power you are praying to can deliver on their promises. Otherwise, praying is all just a useless act on your part if you don't even believe the person or power you are praying to can and will answer you. If you don't have confidence in who you are praying to, it will be totally ineffective, and you may as well not even waste your time praying.

➢ **Prayer is a relationship.** For me, prayer is a relationship with someone whom I trust with every aspect of my life. I trust that He created me, He loves me, and He has my best interest at heart. There is no wavering in my trust in Him in this relationship, and this allows me to freely communicate with Him.

How To Get It:

1. Decide who your higher power is. Like I said before, for me, that is God. I know He's alive, created me, and knows me better than I know myself. I have complete confidence and trust that He can be depended on.

2. Trust your higher power with the outcome of your hard times. I have ideas and preferences on how I hope God answers my prayers, but ultimately, I know the outcome is not for me to control. And I trust that however He answers the prayer, it's for my good.

3. Go back to your mindset of things are happening FOR you, not TO you, and remind yourself of that as you pray through your hard times. Make sure you aren't falling back into a victim mentality.

4. Reflect back on all the other times in your life when God (or your higher power) showed up for you and was faithful. For me, when I'm going through a struggle or experiencing fear or worry, I look back at all the other moments in my life when I was in a bad place or going through a hard time, and God was faithful to see me through it. I remind myself of those hard times and remind myself that He was faithful then, so He will be faithful now.

Checklist

☐ God always answers prayer, just not always in the way we expect Him to.

☐ Prayer is communicating and being dependent on a power higher than yourself.

☐ You must have a relationship with your higher power and confidence that they can deliver on their promises and are capable of seeing you through the hard things.

☐ Decide if you are going to believe in and communicate with a higher power.

☐ Trust God with the outcome of your hard times; don't try to control everything.

☐ Revisit the mindset that things are happening FOR you, not TO you, in Chapter 6.

☐ Reflect back on the ways God has been faithful through other hard times in your life, and use those times to encourage yourself in your present difficulties.

Self-Coaching Questions

✓ Do I trust God in the hard times or do I try to solve problems in my own power?

✓ In what area of my life do I need to let go of control and trust God with the outcome?

✓ Do I fully believe that God (or my higher power) is faithful and competent to see me through my trials?

CHAPTER 15

INTUITION

Follow Your Gut

"Always trust your gut; it knows what your head hasn't figured out yet."

- Anonymous

The new brake lines had been installed and filled with fluid. As we pulled out of that brake shop in San Antonio, TX, we were headed to Arlington, TX. We were just happy this was one of our cheaper repairs, and while we were getting a later start to our trip than planned, we knew we'd still make it to our destination that night…at least that was our plan.

About 20 miles from our destination, driving the busy highways outside of Dallas, TX, I just happened to glance over at Matt and saw a very concerned look on his face. Matt's not one to be very dramatic, so he wasn't saying anything, but I knew something was off. So I asked, "What's wrong? Did we lose our brakes again?" That was the most logical question since we just left the shop hours earlier after getting them fixed. In his monotone voice, he calmly replied, "No, I have my brakes, but I don't have any gears." My heart sank, as I knew exactly what was going on, and I said, "Pull over." We veered off the busy highway and began to troubleshoot, knowing more than likely that we just lost the transmission in our "home".

As we sat stranded along that busy highway at about 9pm at night with our 3 kids, a cat, and no car, we knew we had some decisions to make. It was too late to find a transmission shop that was open and too late to even find out what something like this was going to cost; we would have to wait until morning. But we had to get off the highway for the night, so we knew when the tow truck came, we were headed to a place we were way too familiar with…the Walmart parking lot.

We got some sleep and the next morning I began my phone calls trying to find a shop to fix a transmission on a 37 ft. motorhome. After several calls, I found the place. The problem - it was going to take 3 to 4 days.

We just so happened to have relatives who lived about 45 minutes from where we broke down. One of them came the evening before and drove us to the Walmart while they towed our RV. Then the other graciously welcomed us into their home for a few days while our RV got repaired. So, we packed up our stuff, the kids, and the cat, and headed to their house. The cat peed and pooped in the carrier on Matt's lap as we drove to their house, and he almost got run over on the busy TX highway trying to escape Matt's grasp, but we all made it to their house alive.

What I didn't tell you yet is that several weeks before, we were planning out our route through Texas and wanted to go through Big Bend National Park. Our plan was to go from San Antonio to Big Bend, but as we were planning that trip, I had a gut feeling that we shouldn't take that route. As with my gut feeling most of the time, I'm not sure the exact reason at the time. So I said to Matt, "I can't tell you why, but I don't think we should go to Big Bend after San Antonio. Let's go to Arlington for a few days instead." Matt agreed. He has learned to listen to my gut feelings, as they have guided us well.

Friends, if I would have ignored my gut that day we made the plan, we would have lost our transmission in the middle of a national park with no one we knew around to help us. And that story would have played out a lot differently than it did.

Trusting my gut is one of the most used tools in my toolbox. Some people call it intuition, gut instinct; some will look at it through a spiritual lens and call it the Holy Spirit. In this chapter, for simplicity, I'll be referring to it mostly as "your gut".

Here's what I've learned about Trusting Your Gut:

➢ **Learn to follow it.** If you feel like you are very intuitive and have followed your gut most of your life, then continue to master the skill. If you feel like you aren't even really sure how to follow your gut - you can learn, and there will be some tips in this chapter that will help you get started on that path. *One caution, just because you are choosing to learn to follow your gut, that doesn't mean you are throwing out every other bit of decision-making, wisdom, or logic. The gut just becomes another checkpoint for you to make sure you are on the right path. Think of it as a little yellow "caution" road sign, sometimes it will feel like a red light, and other times it will be like the green light - you'll just know the decision you are making is the right one. It's not either/or, it's both/and.

➢ **Sometimes intuition doesn't make sense to the logical mind.** That doesn't mean it is wrong. There have been many times on my entrepreneurial path when I have made decisions simply on my gut that have made no logical sense, but they were the right decision, and that was confirmed later on through the way something played out. When I'm faced with a decision, and my gut is screaming one thing and logic is screaming another, I master my subconscious of fear and worry and follow my gut. I have found that a lot of times, people know what the right thing is to do, but it's the hard thing, so they tend to reason their way out of following their gut instinct.

➤ **You have to tune out the noise.** In order to be able to know and follow your gut, you have to shut out the background noise, whether that's a well-meaning friend yelling, "Do the safe thing", your own subconscious screaming at you with worry, or something you read on social media. You must be able to block all of that out and tune into what your gut is saying deep inside of you. It may be telling you to "take the risk" or "leave that relationship" or any number of other things that may not be the popular answer.

➤ **Be led by peace**. At the end of the day, the one way I know I'm following my gut and doing the right thing is the peace I have. It's a deep, underlying, below-the-surface peace, a knowing that "this is right". IF I don't have that peace, if I am in turmoil inside, that's my answer. Just like when we were planning our route through Texas, I didn't have all the logic behind why we shouldn't go that route. All I knew is that there was no peace with it, so we chose another route - and there I found my peace.

How To Get It:

1. Remove the outside noise. Get quiet and withdraw from the situation so you can think clearly. Stop asking everyone around you for their opinion. Stop googling everything on the issue. Strip away all the distractions and noise. Use the 4 R's Method we will talk about in Chapter 20 on Decision-Making. Download your free copy at www.lifehacksforhardtimes.com.

2. Master your subconscious. Refer to Chapter 11 - Make sure you aren't reacting out of fear or worry.

3. Ask yourself, "Is the answer inside of me, and I'm trying to reason my way out of it?" Remember, identify the truth.

4. Ask yourself, "What brings me the most peace?"

5. Start paying attention to your gut instinct and build it up, just like you would a muscle. The more you use it, the stronger it gets.

Checklist

☐ Trusting your gut can become one of the most powerful tools in your toolbox.

☐ You can learn to follow your gut, build that muscle, and master the skill.

☐ Sometimes intuition (a gut feeling) doesn't make sense to the logical mind. Make sure you aren't reasoning your way out of what you KNOW deep inside you should do.

☐ Master your subconscious and stop reacting. (Use the 4 R's Method to help with this.)

☐ Tune out the noise and stop asking everyone around you for answers.

☐ Ask yourself powerful questions. (More examples are below in the self-coaching questions.)

☐ Be led by peace.

Self-Coaching Questions

✓ Is the answer inside of me and I'm trying to reason my way out of it?

✓ What brings me the most peace?

✓ If I knew the answer, what would it be?

LIFE HACKS FOR HARD TIMES

CHAPTER 16

FIND JOY IN THE JOURNEY

Life's Not All About the Finish Line

"Wherever you are, be all there." - Jim Elliot

A few weeks after our roach catastrophe in the RV, we had a decision to make because that was our home. We knew we weren't going back to living in the RV, but what next? At that point, we still had no idea where we wanted to live permanently and were still enjoying traveling around, so we made the decision to downsize again, start traveling in our car, and rent fully furnished Airbnbs.

We left Pittsburgh with very little direction on where we were headed, but we knew we'd spend the next week in Northern Alabama and figure it out from there. As the week moved on, we still had no idea where we were headed next...in like 3 days. About 48 hours before we were leaving Alabama, we decided to check options at the beach in Gulf Shores. It was late October by this point, so we were out of the busy vacation season. We happened to find a place available right on the beach and within our budget. I contacted the owner, and she just so happened to live ONLY 20 minutes from where we were staying, so we were able to drive and meet her, get the key, and hand her a check. Out of all the condos available on a site like VRBO, what were the chances she was 20 minutes away?

Two days later, we headed to the beach. We arrived there at about 10pm. I was sick and exhausted. We had literally been living in other people's spaces, that they so graciously offered us, for the past 2 months, pulling our clothes out of a Rubbermaid bin and feeling totally unsettled. I knew we only had this condo for a month, but we were happy to have space to ourselves. When we arrived at the condo, the cleaning crew didn't get the message to clean the condo that day when the other guests checked out. So we arrived to a dirty condo at 10pm with nowhere else to go and no other options other than to start washing bedding and towels and get it to a place where we could at least sleep for the night.

As stressful as all of the uncertainty was over the past 2 months, as frustrating as it was to show up exhausted and sick at this condo and find it in the condition it was, we had a choice to make for the next month, and we chose to absolutely love and appreciate every single day of sitting by the ocean. It was cool, and some days we were the only people there, but the kids played in the sand for hours, while Matt and I sat in our beach chairs with our laptops and built a business.

No, it's not a fun place to be in when you have to constantly ask the question, "Where will I live tomorrow, next week, or next month?" It can get quite exhausting living with that level of uncertainty and can zap one's mental capacity, continually trying to figure it out, but that was life on the road for us, for way longer than we expected. But through it all, one thing we learned to do was "find joy in the journey" and that, my friends, has made all the difference for us.

Here's what I've learned about Finding Joy in the Journey:

➤ **Joy isn't the same as happiness.** Happiness is often dependent on our circumstances. It's an external emotion or euphoria of having what we want. Happiness is about a result. It's inconsistent and temporary. Whereas, joy is an internal act of our will and our contentment, and not based on a result. Rather, it's a consistent foundation in your life. There is nothing wrong with feeling happy, but it's important that we recognize it for what it is. When we try to chase happiness, it's a trap every time. We've all said it in our life: "I'll be happy when…". When you have joy, it's not dependent on your changing and daily circumstances, but rather on the internal perspective that you view life through.

➤ **Shed idealistic expectations.** We can tend to view our lives through a lens of idealistic expectations. We have this picture-perfect marriage in our mind. We plan the perfect vacation. We create this idea of our perfect life. And then when it doesn't play out, we are in a state of constant disappointment and discontentment. Expectations are not bad, but it's important that we set realistic expectations, and understand as we are striving for something, that life's not always going to go as we think it should. The only place the perfect story plays out is in Hollywood. Life is messy but beautiful at the same time.

➤ **Celebrate the journey and destination.** We must learn to celebrate both the journey and the destination. It's also important that when we reach a certain destination, goal, or milestone that we stop and acknowledge it, celebrate it, and reflect on what we learned on the journey to that destination. There is great joy that can be found in any journey, even in the painful ones, just like I told you above with a small portion of our life-on-the-road story. As uncomfortable, exhausted, and over it as we were sometimes, we made so many memories throughout those years, learned so much, and laughed a ton along the way. Don't wait until you get where you think you want to be to start celebrating life, friends. I promise you, it will be anti-climactic, it will probably take you longer to get there than you thought, and you'll probably take a few detours along the way, so decide to celebrate the entire journey.

➢ **Anticipation is a key component.** It's vital that we have something to look forward to, even small things, on a daily basis. Being intentional about having things to look forward to will help bring you joy. This anticipation fuels us to keep going even when it's difficult, helps us enjoy the journey, and refuels us through hard and stressful times. *More on this in the Self-Care Chapter 24.

How To Get It:

1. Stop telling yourself, "I'll be happy when..." or "I'll enjoy my life when...". Those are traps. Decide right now to change your perspective and be intentional about cultivating joy in your life.

2. Go back and review the chapters on Perspective (Chapter 2) and Growth Mindset (Chapter 5) if you need to, as these will help you find joy in your journey.

3. Ask yourself what areas of your life you have idealistic expectations in that are keeping you constantly disappointed and in a state of discontentment. Let go of the "perfect expectations". Give yourself and others some grace.

4. Look at your current journey and ask yourself what ways you can start celebrating things along the way, finding humor, and adding value to others.

5. When you reach a destination or a goal, it is VITAL that you stop and acknowledge it, reflect on what you learned in the process, and decide what takeaways you can take with you for the next journey.

6. Start being intentional about building anticipation into things that bring you joy into your daily life. *More on this in the Refueling Stations Chapter 23, Self-Care Chapter 24, and Seasons Chapter 10.

Checklist

☐ Happiness and joy are two different things. Happiness is an emotion dependent on changing circumstances. Joy is an act of your will that isn't affected by circumstances, but rather by the perspective you view life through.

☐ Stop telling yourself, "I'll be happy when…".

☐ Grab some perspective if you are struggling in this area.

☐ Your idealistic expectations in certain areas of your life are keeping you in a constant state of disappointment and discontentment. Recognize the parts of your life where you are expecting the perfect scenario.

☐ Celebrate the journey; don't wait for the destination to celebrate.

☐ Acknowledge, reflect, and take away valuable insights when you reach your goal or destination. Don't skip this step.

☐ Be intentional about building anticipation in your life. You do this by adding things that bring joy into your daily life.

☐ What can you start celebrating about your current journey (even if it's a painful, stressful one)? Are you growing in an area? What's the lesson in the challenge? Can I build grit or resilience through this that will serve me in the future?

☐ Start acknowledging the destination when you reach it, and grab your takeaways before you move on to the next journey.

☐ Build anticipation into your daily life. It's a force that will help you cultivate joy and refill your soul in the midst of the struggle.

Self-Coaching Questions

- ✓ What brings you joy? (Make a list of as many things you can think of.)
- ✓ How do you want to celebrate this milestone (goal, destination)?
- ✓ What/Who inspires me?
- ✓ Who do I know that has walked through a similar journey that I can find inspiration and hope from?

CHAPTER 17

LET GO

Not Every Battle is Worth the Fight

"Sometimes letting things go is an act of far greater power than holding on."

- Eckhart Tolle

There I was, sitting around a conference table in my attorney's office, hardly believing what I was hearing. I was being told things like, "It is the Christian thing to do to forgive and move on." What?! Someone stole from me and now you want me to just "let it go and come to a peaceful agreement!?" This was not okay with me.

A year prior, my ex-husband and I bought our first house. We were young and stupid (some would say naive), but we are going with stupid. It was the cutest little 650-square-foot ranch house that I couldn't wait to call my own. However, the euphoria of it all quickly faded the minute I opened the mailbox to find a letter from the city, and realized we had been totally screwed over by the realtor, seller, and septic inspector. We had a lagoon in our backyard that was bigger than the house, and it was failing. A whole new septic system needed to be put in. Also, the neighbor who lived behind us was living out his mission on Earth, which was to continue to complain and sue us until it was all fixed. That first realization hit hard, as we realized we were lied to and taken advantage of. I had to make the hard decision to not fight the battle of suing the realtor and previous owner. That was the first hurdle to climb.

As we explored our options, we quickly realized that to put in a system that would pass inspection and shut up the neighbor was going to cost upwards of $20,000. Now, keep in mind that this was a $65,000 house and we were making about $12/ hour at the time. As we were exploring all of these options and trying to figure out how we were going to come up with the money to do this, our good friend jumped in to help. Whew, what a blessing! He was a contractor, and he agreed to help us do the work for next to nothing if we just paid for the materials. This was a no-brainer, so we wrote him a check for $5,000 and waited for the materials. Remember, I said we were stupid?! Now you are agreeing.

A few weeks went by and some of the materials showed up, but Andy was nowhere to be found. After weeks of trying to connect with him, our efforts were in vain, and we realized we were taken advantage of yet again. This time, I wasn't staying silent. I hired a lawyer (without guts) - didn't know that at the time. Another stupid move. And after months of fighting the case, it ended around a table in his office with him, a pastor (without guts), my ex-husband and me, and our former "good" friend. They basically told me I just needed to forgive and forget and move on. I was so angry that day. Now I know why because I know myself, but back then I was just mad, and I vowed that I would never again hire a "Christian" lawyer without guts (and I've kept that promise).

We spent the next year hiring contractors to finish the work, and by the time it was said and done, we had almost $19,000 in that ordeal. We sold the house, put that behind us, and moved on…or so we thought.

Then came the letter to our new house, that the neighbor from behind that old house was suing us again. GAME ON. I had enough. This "house from hell" was still haunting me years after I sold it. So I showed up in court that day with my lawyer (who was helping me with my divorce), and the neighbor didn't show up. Thankfully, this lawyer had some guts and was able to get the judge to dismiss the case in a way that I would never have to fight that battle again.

I don't know what happened to everyone who was involved in this mess, but I do know the septic inspector was hit in the head with a rock and killed on a job. The neighbor died from cancer. And the "good" friends went on to become pastors. I'll let you figure that one out.

The thing I regretted most about this whole situation was the years of my life I wasted sitting in pure anger, worry, and frustration over this mess. I learned so many lessons through this that I have carried with me for years, but I so wish I didn't let it steal my peace and joy in the process. However, these lessons would serve me well when I once again found myself seated around a "virtual" lawyer's table years later - a story you will hear later in this book.

Friends, there are going to be things that happen in our life that suck. Things that want to steal our peace, time, energy, and joy. Sometimes there are battles worth fighting - like the one I fought to regain my mental and emotional health. And sometimes there are battles that we just need to let go of.

Here's what I've learned about Letting Go:

➤ **Letting go isn't a sign of weakness.** I used to fight every battle. I mean every single battle because if I just let it go, that would be weak, and I wasn't interested in looking weak. But what I've learned is that letting go sometimes takes more courage, more guts, and more trust than holding on and fighting.

➤ **Your comfort zone isn't keeping you safe.** Sometimes we stay in bad relationships, toxic jobs, or put up with things we should never tolerate because it's what we are used to. If you start having a headache every day, for the first couple of weeks it's annoying, and you want it to go away, but after a few weeks, you start to get used to just living with a headache every day and forget what it's like to not have a headache. So you accept it, adapt and move on. Your comfort zone, as unhealthy as it is, isn't keeping you safe. Just because you've learned to live in that toxic or abusive relationship for decades, doesn't make it right. Just because you don't know what life would be like without it, doesn't mean you shouldn't leave it. It's important that when you need to let go of something, you have the courage to do it. You may have heard the saying, "When you straddle the fence, something gets hurt." You can't hold onto bitterness and anger while striving to become your best self and live with joy! You can't have both. You have to let go to grab onto something better. You can't keep trying to control everything in your life while at the same time trusting and having peace. It's one or the other.

➢ **The only thing and person you can ever control is YOU.** If you are trying to control everything and everyone in your life, you are living in codependency. This book is not meant to be a comprehensive resource for codependency - there are plenty of tools out there on this. For years, I thought codependency described people who were living with alcoholics and enabling them to stay in their addiction, or someone who was in an abusive relationship and putting up with it. So I always thought codependency isn't a struggle of mine! And then came the day when my mindset coach opened my own eyes to the ways I was living in codependency simply by trying to control the outcome of things and control the way others responded to me by framing everything I said to them in a way that tried to manipulate their response, and I didn't even realize I was doing it! Whew! To say that it hit me like a ton of bricks is an understatement. I think I literally cried for 3 days straight and could hardly function, but on the other side of it was the most freeing feeling I've ever had. I can't, and don't, need to control other people's responses to me, the outcome of a situation, or anything else. I simply need to show up, speak my truth, and trust God with the rest. Friends, can I tell you how freeing that was for me to LET GO of control? If you can relate, it's time you stop trying to control everything and start showing up fully engaged. Trust the process, divorce the outcome.

How To Get It:

1. First, evaluate if the situation you are dealing with is something you need to fight through or let go of. There is a difference between a relationship that needs course-corrected, like Matt and my marriage early on; we didn't need to divorce. We needed to start to understand ourselves better and, in turn, understand each other better, work on our communication skills, and fight for the marriage we have today. Then there are the relationships that are toxic, like abusive relationships. Those aren't things you are meant to fight through; those are things you should let go of.

2. Ask yourself, "Is my hard time because I won't let go of something and am afraid to get out of my comfort zone?" Even if your comfort zone is not comfortable.

3. Ask powerful questions:
   a) Is fighting through this situation moving me towards my values, purpose, and vision? Or is it moving me away from them?
   b) Am I pushing so hard because I need to be resilient in this situation, or because I don't want to look weak by letting it go?
   c) Am I trying to control the outcome instead of letting go and trusting?

4. Use the emotions that you are feeling in the situation as indicators (refer to Chapter 18) and gain understanding about yourself in the process.

5. Decide to get out of your comfort zone, make hard decisions that align with your values and move you toward your purpose, and when you know you need to let go, don't prolong the process. Do it.

Checklist

☐ Know which battles are worth fighting and which ones are not.

☐ Letting go is actually a sign of great strength, not weakness. It's often way harder to let go than it is to hold on.

☐ Your comfort zone isn't keeping you safe.

☐ The only thing and person you can control is YOU.

☐ If you are trying to control everything and everyone, you are living in codependency. Be intentional about walking free from that.

☐ Evaluate the situation you are in to determine if it's something you need to fight through or something you need to let go. Do this by asking powerful questions.

☐ Use your emotions as indicators and learn from them. Don't let them dictate your reactions.

☐ Decide to get out of your comfort zone, let go, and grab onto the things that align with your values and move you toward your purpose.

Self-Coaching Questions

✓ Is my hard time because I am refusing to let go?
✓ Am I trying to control the outcome of the situation instead of letting go and trusting the process?
✓ What is one way I can better my life by leaving my comfort zone?

CHAPTER 18

EMOTIONS

Thermometer Not Thermostat

"To master your emotions is not to suppress them. It is to process them with diligence, and express them with intelligence." - Kam Taj

S itting in my car, and on the other end of the phone, my mom says, "John (financial advisor) needs to reach you because you and Matt were designated as beneficiaries on Jane's will." I was dumbfounded. Jane was a great friend for years. Matt and I did a lot of work at her house. We included her in our family holiday celebrations and birthday parties, but neither of us was expecting to be listed as beneficiaries on her will. My first thought after coming off a very rough time financially was, "This could end up being a huge blessing." As we started discussing the numbers with her financial advisor, John, we realized that the money that was left to us could help us clean up a mess and move forward with some financial stability that we hadn't had in a few years.

Just a few weeks after this great news, we realized this wasn't going to be as easy as we thought, as the executor for her estate wasn't handling things the way they were supposed to be handled. As we endeavored to get the death certificate, we realized she had "locked down" all our ways to get the death certificate (which wasn't proper legal protocol, but integrity wasn't her motive). Matt and I are pretty resourceful, so we figured out how to apply for the death certificate and prove our validity to receive the certificate directly from the state. So it took some time (this is the government we are talking about), but we got it! We thought, "This is over! - she thought she had us, but she didn't realize who she was dealing with!" Feeling very satisfied with our efforts and hopeful, we submitted the paperwork to the insurance company and figured we'd have our check within a couple of weeks.

Then the call came. I'll never forget that evening the New York City lawyer rang Matt's phone and informed us that the executor, let's call her Gertrude, filed a federal lawsuit with the insurance agency and put Matt and me on there as defendants. She let us know that no money could be paid out until this lawsuit was resolved. To say I was angry would be a slight understatement. We got off that phone call, and I went into a pure rage (not the kind where I was going to hurt anyone), but the tears that flooded and the emotions I felt inside were ones of anger, hate, and rage. As I stood in my kitchen and let words fly and tears stream, Matt just let me get it out. He offered to hold me, but he knew better than to tell me to calm down. He knew exactly why I was reacting the way I did, and so did I.

At this point in my life, I knew myself so well that I knew every trigger this situation was hitting on and knew the emotions I was feeling were completely validated based on the situation. I was not apologizing for anything I felt. But I also knew that I couldn't control anyone but ME. I was responsible for how I handled this and how I let this situation affect me.

So, the battle continued. After calming down for a night, I was thinking clearly, understanding my emotions, but knew no matter how this ended, there were a few things that were important to me. At this point, I wasn't attached to the outcome (remember, we aren't living with codependency anymore), but I was committed to a couple of things. First, I was committed to the fact that Matt and I would stand for justice, we would do everything in our power to carry out our friend's wishes, and we would not roll over. Secondly, I was also determined that while we were going to see this through to the end, we would not let it steal or take away ANY of our peace, time, or hard-earned money. So we made a decision that day that we would not hire a lawyer and pay those fees, we would not spend time or energy being upset about this, and we would trust God with the outcome.

We spent the next year answering lawyers' letters or calls when we needed to. We would simply state the truth and inform them we were not going away. Matt and John kept telling me that there was no way we couldn't win this case because everything was in writing, and the law was the law, and they threw out big words to me like, "If Gertrude wins this case, it will set the precedent for other insurance claims". But I knew it wasn't that cut and dry. My gut was telling me differently. It was telling me, "This is a corrupt system, and if we get the wrong judge, this will not end like they are saying."

Gertrude played the part of the coward throughout this whole process and never once spoke to us directly. Then, the day came when we had to talk to her lawyer, the NY lawyer, the judge, and who knows who else was on that virtual call. It didn't take me long to realize we were dealing with a judge who was not looking at the law or truth, but only what felt fair in his eyes. He also was in some sort of backdoor relationship with the lawyers. As we sat on that call and he lied, manipulated, and gaslighted us, neither Matt nor I reacted. But we did respond with very direct truth, which they didn't appreciate.

To make a long story short, Jane's sister was also involved in this case, which was upsetting to watch her, as she continued to grieve her sister's death while having to be put through all of this because of someone's pure greed. In the process of it all, Matt and I knew that no matter what happened with us and the money that was owed us, we needed to make sure her sister was taken care of and that she received everything Jane left for her.

After 18 months of fighting this battle, we won that case, didn't pay a dime in lawyers fees for anyone, blessed her sister, and stood for justice. But the bigger win in all of this was the fact that, throughout the 18-month process, unlike my septic story, this situation didn't steal our peace, our joy, or our energy. We recognized it for what it was and allowed our emotions to be indicators, not dictators in our life.

Emotions are powerful forces, friends, they are part of life. If we let them dictate our life, they will ruin us, but if we let them inform us, they can be used to gain self-awareness, make better decisions, and truly enjoy an emotion-filled life.

Here's what I've learned about Emotions:

> **Emotions will always be part of life.** We are human beings, we feel deeply. You can ignore and stuff your emotions all day long, but they aren't going away. Emotions in themselves are not right or wrong, good or bad. They are simply emotions. I think so many times we have been conditioned to believe that if we are sad, mad, offended, angry, and so on, that those are wrong and bad emotions, so we ignore or stuff those emotions, which doesn't end well.

> **Emotions are meant to be indicators, not dictators in our life.** A thermometer can only tell you what the temperature is in a room. A thermostat, on the other hand, can cause the temperature to change. Your emotions should be like the thermometer, where they give you indications on what is going on inside of you, but they shouldn't be a thermostat, where they drive your decisions. Your emotions should simply be data to help you make decisions, understand yourself better, or respond to situations.

> **It's important to understand more than the base-level emotions you are feeling.** How many times do you ask someone, "How are you?" And they respond with something like, "I'm good." "I'm angry." "I'm upset." "I'm okay." It's important that we dig below the surface of a base-level emotion like, "I'm angry." Are you offended, irritated, overwhelmed, or defensive? By being more specific about your emotions, you can get to the root of what's really triggering you or making you feel that way. This awareness helps you truly understand how you feel and why it's affecting you. Then you can effectively articulate and communicate it with others. This

114

allows them to hear and understand what you are really saying. Without it, there is a gap in communication. It's hard to bring resolution to a situation when each party isn't even sure what the root problem is. If a friend tells you, "I'm mad at you", the other person doesn't even really understand what they did to make you mad, and whether they apologize or not, it doesn't really get resolved. But if that same friend tells you that they felt taken advantage of when they spent all weekend helping you paint your house, and you didn't even offer to feed them a meal or say thank you, that is a whole lot clearer explanation of why they are "mad" at you than just, "I'm mad at you." Now you understand why they feel the way they do and why it's upsetting them, and you can understand where they are coming from and how your action affected them. Then resolution can truly come. That's the importance of digging below the base-level emotions.

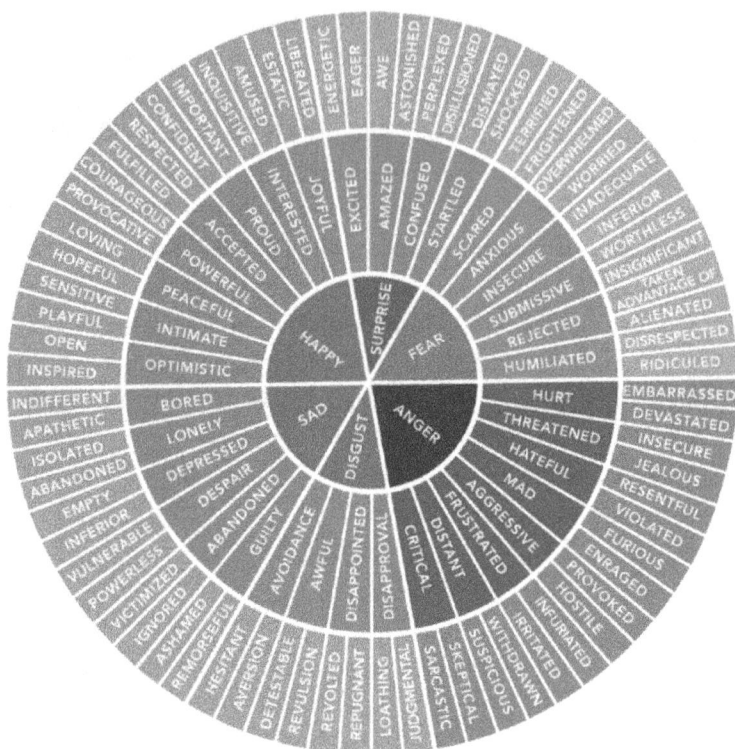

Emotions Wheel

For detailed instructions on using the Emotions Wheel, download the free resources for this book at www.lifehacksforhardtimes.com.

> ➢ **Understand the difference between reacting vs. responding.**
> When we allow our emotions to drive us, we tend to react to the situation and make emotional decisions based on worry, fear, excitement, instant gratification, or any other emotion. Those decisions aren't necessarily aligned with our values, moving us toward our purpose or helping us keep our priorities. Instead, if we withdraw from the situation, ask ourselves what the emotions are trying to tell us, and then rethink the situation, we can respond to the situation without the emotions driving our response. There may

be emotions tied to your response BUT they aren't driving the response, and that's the difference. (4R's Method download will help you nail this!)

How To Get It:

1. Acknowledge the emotions - don't stuff them, ignore them or react to them. Just acknowledge them.

2. Retreat from the situation before you react. This doesn't have to be a long process; I do this every day in my life, and sometimes it's a 30-second process, and other times, it's a deeper issue and takes longer.

3. Dig below the surface. Use the emotion wheel on this page (and in the free resources) to get below the base level emotion and find out what's really triggering you, so you can understand it better yourself and articulate to others better.

4. Ask yourself, "What are these emotions telling me?" Make a list.

5. Something else that is helpful is making a list of "How I Feel". Maybe you are going through a rough time right now - I would encourage you to get a piece of paper and just bullet point how you are feeling. Then, on the other side of the paper write, "How I Want to Feel" and bullet how you want to feel. This will help you get your emotions out and also get clarity on where you are headed, and what decisions need to be made to move you from one side of the page to the other.

6. Decide how to respond to what the emotions are telling you. Do you need to let yourself feel them and let them pass? Set a boundary? Change the way you are doing something? Speak your truth to someone?

Checklist

☐ Emotions will always be a part of your life. They aren't good or bad, wrong or right.

☐ Emotions are meant to be indicators, not dictators in your life. Let them be a thermometer, not a thermostat.

☐ Acknowledge the emotions you are feeling.

☐ Ask yourself, "What are these emotions telling me?"

☐ Dig below the base level emotions to what you are truly feeling inside and gain clarity as to why you feel that way. Use the Emotion Wheel to do this.

☐ Retreat from the situation instead of immediately reacting.

☐ Start responding to situations in your life through the filter of what aligns with your values, purpose and priorities.

☐ Compare how you actually feel vs. how you want to feel in a situation.

☐ Decide what intentional actions to take based on the insight you gained from your emotions.

Self-Coaching Questions

✓ How do I want to show up in this situation?
✓ What are these emotions telling me?
✓ What's really going on beneath the surface?
✓ If I wasn't reacting to the emotion, what would the decision be?

CHAPTER 19

LAUGHTER

Why Do Hamburgers Fly South for the Winter?

"Laughter is an instant vacation." - Milton Berle

I t's about 8pm in the evening, and I'm sitting at my kitchen table in my RV doing a Zoom meeting when I hear Matt slapping something behind me and stomping his foot. Inside my head I'm thinking, "What in the world is going on? It's not like Matt to be making a bunch of noise while I'm in a meeting, especially right behind my head." But I just kept my composure and continued on. I got off the call and Matt said, "We have a problem." I responded with, "You think so? What in the world was all that noise while I was in my meeting?" He's like, "We have roaches in the RV." Not what I was expecting or wanting to hear. They were crawling out from under our washer/dryer unit and eating our cat's food. Gross. We decided to see how bad it was. We snuck back to our bedroom, shut all of the lights off, and watched an episode of Seinfeld. Then we got back up, snuck out to the kitchen, and flipped the lights on, and much to our dismay, we saw way too many roaches scatter AND fly. I had enough. I woke up the kids, who were already asleep in the living room, and said, "Grab a change of clothes and anything else you can't live without, and we are out of here." We called some good friends - by this point, it was pushing 11pm - and showed up at their house and crashed on their living room floor until the morning.

I hate bugs. Especially infesting bugs. There was no way I was about to go back and live in that. Thankfully, we could crash with our friends for the next couple of weeks while we figured it out. We tried setting out glue traps to trap them; the cat was unfazed and was no help in killing them. We finally brought in an exterminator. I told him, "These roaches fly", to which he responded, "Roaches don't fly," as one zipped past his head. He asked where we traveled last because "these are not Pennsylvania roaches." We told him Texas, and that helped clarify where we picked these disgusting things up from. They had hibernated in our RV all winter because it was so cold in PA and now they were coming out again.

He informed us that we had all the life cycles going on there, and it was going to take several weeks to kill them all off. And, as he proceeded to tear through my entire RV and rip apart everything I owned, (which wasn't much, but it was all I had), he put poison and bait down. Something else no one knew at the time was that it was a very scary fear of mine for people to mess with my belongings, so him ripping apart my space triggered things inside of me no one else knew about; so I fought off fear and panic in the midst of it all. And then, he told us to keep an eye on them and watch their behavior over the next several weeks. To which I told him, "There is no way I'm going to live in this RV with these bugs, the poison, and the mess." And he said, "Well if this was your house, would you just move out?" To which I said, "This IS my house, and YES I'm moving out!" And I burst into tears. Matt slowly moved me aside and figured he better take over the conversation. So he kindly thanked the guy and sent him on his way. I had to go back in there to get a few things out. As I was waiting for Matt to finish showering, these roaches all of a sudden became more active, like they were drunk from the poison. They were running everywhere, all in different directions. One came running towards me, and Matt is yelling, "Babe, kill it! You got this!" And, as I literally screamed, cried, and prayed to Jesus all in one loud breath, I tried to smash that thing with my flip flop, and even after crushing it and taking off its head, it still ran around!

I'm about to gag just writing this. Needless to say, that ended our RVing days. There is more to that story, but that's for another time.

Friends, this story is hilarious now, and when we think back on it, in the moment, we laugh.

Here's what I've learned about Laughter:

➢ **It is an AMAZING medicine.** Now, I'm not a doctor, and not giving you any medical advice here, legal advice or any other advice in this entire book - use your own brain and judgment. But some of the stats I saw from the Mayo Clinic on the benefits of laughter were:
  o Stimulates many different organs.
  o Activates and relieves your stress response.
  o Soothes tension.
  o Improves your immune system.
  o Relieves pain.
  o Increases personal satisfaction.
  o Improves your mood.
  The Bible even says in Proverbs that a "Merry heart doeth good like a medicine…"

➢ **Just because you are laughing through a hard time, doesn't mean you are in denial.** Sometimes we think that because we are going through a hard time, we have to be somber, serious, and heavy-hearted because if we are light-hearted, laugh or crack a joke, we don't realize the gravity of the situation we are in. For me, that has not been the case. I have laughed through many hard times and in no way was oblivious to my hard time. Just as the quote above says, "Laughter is an instant vacation." I love that. Laughter clears your mind, it takes you away from the struggle, even if it's for a moment, and gives you an injection of positive emotion that you so desperately need in your time of struggle.

> **You may not laugh at every point throughout the struggle.** Let me explain this. Sometimes there are things you just can't laugh at in the moment of it happening. When we realized we had roaches in our RV, I was not laughing…at all. But while going through it, in the middle of it, and after it, we have laughed many times over about this. When our RV broke down with a bad starter, we were able to laugh in that moment, knowing we may as well make the most of that moment. If you are given a serious diagnosis, you're probably not going to bust out laughing in your doctor's office. But, through the struggle, finding ways to laugh in the midst of it will help the healing process. The point is, if you wait until there is no struggle to laugh, that will never happen.

How To Get It:

1. Have people in your life who make you laugh, especially if you are generally more serious. You need to find people in your life who can bring humor to your life.

2. Give yourself permission to laugh. Just because the hard time you are in is serious, it's hard, and it's exhausting, it's still so important that you allow yourself to laugh, even if it's watching a 5-minute hilarious video on YouTube.

3. Be intentional about making laughter part of your life. Different things make different people laugh. Matt loves watching stupid, funny movies and repeating lines with other people. That doesn't do much for me because I get the stupid part, but not the funny part. But I find other ways to laugh, and love to laugh. We laugh through our HARD times all the time. It's an integral part of our life. If you lived with us for one day, you would laugh so much, even in the midst of our struggles. I have no doubt it's one of the tools that has kept us going through some very, very hard times.

Checklist

☐ Laughter is an amazing medicine - it feeds your body and soul.

☐ Remember, just because you are laughing through a hard time doesn't mean you are in denial.

☐ There may be points in the struggle that you can't laugh at, but find ways to laugh at other points throughout or after the struggle.

☐ Get people in your life who make you laugh. If you don't have them, go find them.

☐ Give yourself permission to laugh. Life is too short to be serious all the time.

☐ Be intentional about making laughter a part of your life.

Self-Coaching Questions

✓ Who in my life makes me laugh?
✓ What areas of my life am I taking too seriously?
✓ When is the last time I have laughed so hard it hurts?
✓ What's one way I can incorporate laughter into my life on a consistent basis?

And by the way…Hamburgers fly south for the winter so they don't freeze their buns off!
You can thank Matt for that (stupid) joke.

CHAPTER 20

DECISION-MAKING

No Decision Is Still a Decision

"You cannot make progress without making decisions." - Jim Rohn

About 3 weeks after my unexpected visit to the mental health ward, I was walking through my new house. At this point, I was still unpacking boxes and getting settled when a thought popped into my mind, "It's time to move back home." Say what?! St. Louis was home now. I had built a life here and, even though I was having to rebuild part of that life as a young, single, divorced woman, I still had a job I loved, had started a professional organizing business, and had some amazing friendships. The fact was that I had no intention of moving back to Pittsburgh, I mean I literally just closed on this house 3 weeks prior. But I knew that feeling…that gut feeling that's led me my entire life. And I knew that it wasn't some harebrained idea I just came up with because it wasn't even on my radar.

So, I called my dad and said, "I'm coming home", which was music to his ears. So within a month of signing papers to own my new house, it was back on the market, and in another month, I would be signing another set of papers to sell it. My parents and a dear friend drove out and helped me move back to start the next chapter of my life.

That move was so bittersweet. I left people and a life I loved in St. Louis but was excited to start over and build a life I love. At the time, I had no idea how this decision would affect the rest of my life; I just knew it was the right decision. That one decision led me to Matt. What I didn't realize at the time was that he was just the person I would need in the years to follow as life hit hard and I found myself fighting to survive. God saw it, and He knew I would need a partner who was stronger than I am to withstand the storms ahead and who would be loyal through it all and see us through to the other side.

We all make decisions every day of our life. A lot of those decisions are insignificant in the scope of life, but there are times when we have to make decisions that will forever change the trajectory of our lives.

Here's what I've learned about Decision-Making:

- ➤ **Decisions are and will always be a part of your life.** Sometimes people struggle to make decisions, and they can be even more challenging to make in the midst of hard times because emotions are elevated, there is usually more at stake, and you are generally facing uncertainty, which most human beings don't like.

- ➤ **We sometimes get stuck making them when there is more at stake.** When you are deciding where you want to eat dinner Saturday night, there is little at stake. Worst case, you may get a bad meal, subpar service or spend more than you wanted. But when it comes to hard times and decisions that affect your health, the future of your family, your relationships, your career or business, your bank account, and other people, the pressure is greater to make the right decision. So, a lot of times you won't make a decision, sometimes even tolerate something you need to move on from because the risk is too great.

➢ **We are afraid of making mistakes.** When fear of failure and making mistakes is part of your thought process, that will cripple you from making decisions because you are so afraid that you'll make the wrong one. That's why it's so important that you address your fixed mindset and shift to a growth mindset that embraces challenges and learns from failure. Failure is not something to be feared, it's a great teacher.

Being able to make confident decisions in the midst of a hard time is a tool that will serve you very well. Here's…

How To Get It:

1. You need to first get perspective on the decision that needs to be made. Ask yourself, "What is the worst-case scenario?" For example, per my story above, I had to say to myself, what is the worst-case scenario if I sell my house and move back to Pittsburgh and it was the wrong decision? Then I pack up and move back to St. Louis and buy another house. When you can get the decision at hand in perspective, it helps take the "scary/unknown" out of it. No matter how bad the worst-case scenario is, it's important that you identify it so you know what you are working with.

2. You must take the emotion (Chapter 18) out of it and master your subconscious brain (Chapter 11). Use the tools I gave you in those chapters, but it's imperative that you are not operating out of fear, worry, or panic.

3. List all your options. Remember, way back in Chapter 4 when we talked about options - go back and review that and list every option you have in this situation (don't filter them yet - just list them).

4. Now, look at your values and priorities and filter those options through them. If there are options on that list that do not align with your values - cross them off. *For more specific coaching to help

you identify your core values, check out my latest workshops and group-coaching bundles at www.lifehacksforhardtimes.com.

5. Now, filter your remaining options through the lens of your purpose and vision. Remember, your purpose and vision act as your compass. So ask yourself, "Which of these options will move me toward my purpose and vision?" If some of the options are moving you away from your purpose, those probably aren't the options you want to choose.

BONUS TIP: Years ago, my very first life coach taught me a skill I have used to this day and have made it into a special report for you to download at www.lifehacksforhardtimes.com. It's called "The 4 R's Method: How to Make Better Decisions Every Time". This one method alone has helped me make thousands of decisions over the years and has helped me to respond instead of reacting to challenges, problems, and opportunities I am facing. Go grab a copy and use it with the tools I gave you above, and decision-making will become so much simpler for you!

Checklist

- ☐ Decisions are and will always be a part of your life. No decision is still a decision.
- ☐ You may get stuck making decisions when you feel there is more at stake and/or you're afraid of making a mistake.
- ☐ It's important that you shift to a growth mindset and stop fearing failure.
- ☐ Get perspective on the situation.
- ☐ Identify the worst-case scenario.
- ☐ Take the emotions out of the decision-making process and master your subconscious mind.
- ☐ List ALL the options. (Chapter 4)
- ☐ Weigh out the options against your values and priorities and eliminate any options that don't align with your values.

- ☐ Filter the remaining list of options through your purpose and vision.
- ☐ Go download your free bonus report, "The 4 R's Method".
- ☐ Confidently and courageously make better decisions without fear that move you toward your values, purpose, and vision!

Self-Coaching Questions:

- ✓ If you look back a few years from now, what will you wish you had done in this current season? *You can change the time frame on that question to make it make sense for the decision you are trying to make - EX: If you look back a month from now…
- ✓ What are your options?
- ✓ Does this decision move me toward my purpose and vision or away from it?
- ✓ Does this decision line up with my values and priorities?
- ✓ If you knew the answer, what would it be?

CHAPTER 21

BOUNDARIES

"No" Is a Complete Sentence

"You are not required to set yourself on fire to keep others warm." - Anonymous

I 'll never forget my first meeting with my soon-to-be first Life Coach I would ever hire. I sat across the table from her at our local Starbucks, looked her straight in the eyes, and said, "I need help or I'm about to fire every client of mine, end all of my relationships, and ignore the world." She looked at me and said, "You need some boundaries, and I can help."

I had just moved back from St. Louis a few months prior. I was dating Matt at the time, working a full-time job, and running a part-time business, along with exploring the possibilities of starting an ice cream shop and real estate investment business with my parents. I was passionate about rebuilding my life and was determined I was going to do it quickly! I was all in! What I didn't realize was that in the process of conquering the world, I would fail to set any boundaries, try to be all things to all people, and let whoever wanted to take advantage of me.

I had myself at a point of near burnout, and I knew I needed help. So I hired Nancy that day. Over the next several months, she and I worked closely together, and she gave me tools that I continue to use to this day to keep healthy relationships, have margin in my life, and make better decisions. One of those tools quickly became my best friend...BOUNDARIES...and we've been friends ever since.

Psychology Today sums it up well, "Boundaries can be defined as the limits we set with other people, which indicate what we find acceptable and unacceptable in their behavior towards us. The ability to know our boundaries generally comes from a healthy sense of self-worth, or valuing yourself in a way that is not contingent on other people or the feelings they have toward you."

Here's what I've learned about Boundaries:

> **Boundaries don't have to be brick walls.** A lot of times people have misconceptions about boundaries. They think they have to put up brick walls and turn everyone away in their lives. They think if they set a boundary, they'll lose all their friends and people won't like them. Let me tell you, friends, the only relationships you will lose by setting boundaries are the ones you need to lose because the people who won't respect your boundaries don't deserve to be in your life in the first place. Boundaries don't have to be all or nothing. Let me give you an example: I once had a client, and she was expressing how she was invited to a baby shower for one of her family members. She really wanted to support this family member, but because of her own struggles with infertility, she didn't feel that she could handle attending the baby shower while keeping her own emotions in check. So, she thought her two options were: she could set a boundary and say, "I'm not coming," or she could attend the shower and deal with the heartache that would follow. However, when we dug into it more, we uncovered another option (see that we are back to options). She ended up telling her that she loved her

and was excited for her, and she wanted to celebrate with her, but she didn't think she could handle the group celebration, so they decided to get together at another time to celebrate, just the two of them. Do you see how she set a boundary? But she still was able to support someone she loved while standing up for herself. Boundaries don't always have to be brick walls, sometimes they can be clear plexiglass or they can act as a yield sign or a detour.

➤ **Hard times can be brought on because you don't have clear, healthy boundaries.** Just like my example in the story above, I brought on my own hard times because I didn't clearly define my boundaries with my clients, my co-workers, or my family. I allowed my crude co-workers to talk to me any way they wanted. I allowed my clients to keep me longer than they paid for, and call me after hours for unimportant things. I allowed my family to make their problems my problems. This put me in a place of feeling totally tapped out and quite frankly, angry because my fear of being taken advantage of was being poked all the time. In my story in the first chapter, my boundaries were being broken physically, emotionally, and sexually all the time while in that messed-up relationship, and I had no one to blame but ME. I brought on my hard times by my own poor decisions and lack of self-worth.

➤ **We teach people how to treat us.** I have learned that people will take you as far as you let them take you. You and I train people how to treat or not treat us. If you allow someone to trample on all of your boundaries or you don't set any boundaries to begin with, people will take full advantage of you. If you let the energy vampires in your life suck all your time and energy, and answer the phone every time they call, guess what? They'll keep calling, and they'll keep draining you of all of your energy and time. We train people how to treat us by putting healthy, clear boundaries in place AND then enforcing those boundaries. This will take some effort, but it is worth it.

➤ **Don't take on other people's problems.** The easiest way to identify if you are doing this and then stop doing this is by looking at what your area of responsibility is and what other people's area is.

The more you can stay in your own area of responsibility and not try to fix everyone's problems and be everyone's bleeding heart, the better off you will be. Especially during hard times, the last thing you need to be doing is taking on everyone else's problems. I call this staying in your "R" for short.

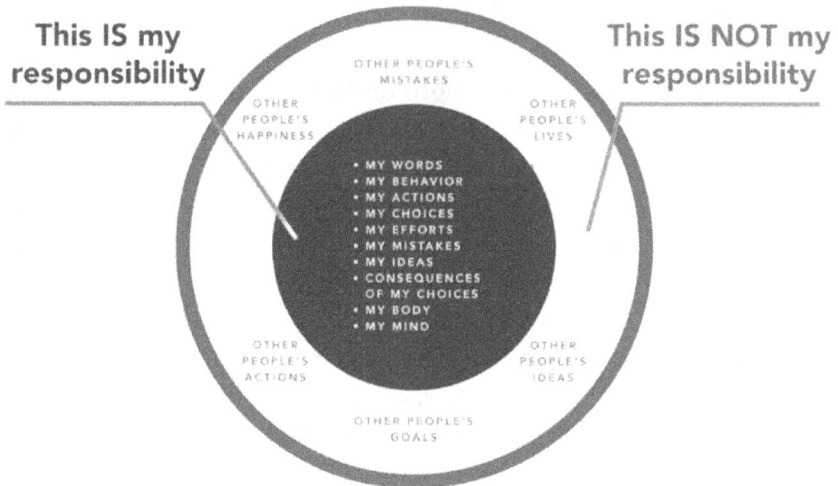

This IS my responsibility

This IS NOT my responsibility

OTHER PEOPLE'S MISTAKES

OTHER PEOPLE'S HAPPINESS

OTHER PEOPLE'S LIVES

- MY WORDS
- MY BEHAVIOR
- MY ACTIONS
- MY CHOICES
- MY EFFORTS
- MY MISTAKES
- MY IDEAS
- CONSEQUENCES OF MY CHOICES
- MY BODY
- MY MIND

OTHER PEOPLE'S ACTIONS

OTHER PEOPLE'S IDEAS

OTHER PEOPLE'S GOALS

Circle of Responsibility

For a copy of this diagram, download the free resources for this book at www.lifehacksforhardtimes.com.

How To Get It:

1. Ask yourself if you have any boundaries in place? If not, you need to start there and set healthy boundaries. Some steps to help you do this are:
    a) Understand your purpose and why you are here (Chapter 9).
    b) Then determine what you have to give to others and what you are willing to give based on your purpose and priorities (you can't do everything).
    c) Determine what your boundaries are based on your core values. For example: One of my core values is Time - I can't ever get it back, so I am very selective with how I spend it. If I feel someone

or something is wasting my time, I am quick to set that boundary and move on before I am at a point of burnout.

    d)   For a more in-depth discussion on this topic - check out the book, *Boundaries*, by Henry Cloud and John Townsend.

2.   Stop and ask if the hard time you are experiencing was brought on by having no boundaries or letting others cross your boundaries. If it was brought on by doing things outside of your "R", then you need to stop and give the problem back to the person it belongs to.

3.   Evaluate if the things you are currently doing in your life are in your "R" or if they are outside of it. Start being aware of when others try to pull you outside of your "R" or when you are going outside of your "R", and get back to your "R".

4.   One thing that helped me immensely when I started setting and keeping healthy boundaries was to journal about it every single day. At the end of every day, I would take 10-15 minutes and journal in what ways I kept my boundaries that day, what empowered me to keep them, and how I felt. And I would journal in what ways my boundaries were broken that day, what caused them to be broken, and how it made me feel. This gave me great awareness of the areas I needed to improve in, and kept me accountable to myself as I was building this new habit.

Checklist

☐   Boundaries are limits we set with other people in our lives - in all areas: emotional, physical, mental, spiritual, intellectual, and sexual.

☐   Boundaries don't have to be rigid, brick walls. You may have stricter boundaries with certain people in your life because they need them, and you may have looser boundaries with other people in your life because you know they will respect you, and you can trust them. It's not always all or nothing.

☐   Hard times can be brought on because you don't have clear, healthy boundaries or aren't enforcing them.

☐ You train people how to treat or not treat you, so make sure you are consistent.

☐ Taking on other people's problems and areas of responsibility breaks their boundaries and will lead you to a place of burnout.

☐ If you don't have healthy boundaries in place in your life, the first place to start is to set them.

☐ Boundaries, by Henry Cloud and John Townsend, is a great book if you want to dive deeper into this subject.

☐ Ask yourself if the hard time you are in is because of a lack of boundaries or if you are in someone else's area of responsibility, trying to take on their problems.

☐ Start reflective journaling (Chapter 22) on your daily takeaways from setting and breaking boundaries so you can gain clarity and self-awareness to continue to make healthy boundary setting a part of your life.

Self-Coaching Questions:

✓ Do I value myself in a way that isn't contingent on other people's thoughts or feelings about me?

✓ Is there a particular struggle I'm having right now because I haven't set or enforced boundaries?

✓ What is my next step in setting healthy boundaries?

✓ Do I spend the majority of my time and energy in my "R" OR do I spend it worrying about and fixing someone else's "R"?

CHAPTER 22

REFLECTIVE JOURNALING

This Is Not an English Paper

"Reflective thinking turns experience into insight." - John C. Maxwell

A s I sat at my computer, with tears streaming down my face, my fingers banging at the keyboard, I recounted the story of my miscarriage to my family and friends. I realized as I wrote the story, it did a couple of things for me. It made me realize all the signs God was giving me along the way as He was preparing me for what was about to happen. It made me humbled and grateful that I wasn't blindsided by this. It confirmed my ability to follow my gut instinct and how it was leading me in the right way through the entire journey. I also realized that getting my emotions and feelings out on paper was healing in its own way. Being able to get below the surface emotions, I realized why certain things affected me the way they did. And being able to share my story with others, from a place of vulnerability, I was able to offer others hope in the midst of their own grief and pain. If I tried to recount that story now, I could give you the details, but not necessarily get back to the emotions and thoughts I had in that moment, but because I recounted it right after it happened, those moments are forever recorded on paper.

Here's what I've learned about Reflective Journaling:

➢ **Reflective journaling doesn't have to read like middle school drama.** Just because you journal doesn't mean it needs to sound like a middle school drama that you would write in your 12-year-old diary. I've had people hesitate to adopt the practice of journaling because they look at it as a strictly emotional, reactionary tool. You can certainly write that way in a moment of deep pain, hurt or excitement. But that's not its only purpose.

➢ **Key word in this chapter is REFLECTIVE.** It is important that we journal in order to reflect on a situation to gain insight into it. Reflecting helps us take the experience we just had to a new level and grow and learn from it. It's intentional. I love the point John Maxwell makes that reflection turns experience into insight. Don't waste your experiences, friends. Whether they are good or bad, start reflecting and gaining insight from them.

➢ **It serves several purposes.**
  o Forces you to put your feelings into words and dig below the surface-level emotion (refer to Chapter 18 on Emotions), which allows you to see triggers and fears clearly.
  o Helps you recognize what is going on underneath the surface level emotions.
  o No experience is wasted - you can use every experience to learn and grow.
  o When you write it down, it's easier to look back on and remember. It anchors those positive neurons in your brain.
  o Next time you encounter a similar obstacle, you are able to look back on that experience and have the tools and insights to make confident decisions.
  o Increases your self-awareness in all situations.

How To Get It:

1. Do not overthink journaling or try to do it perfectly. Your high school English teacher isn't going to find your journal and grade it. It doesn't even need to sound intelligent or be grammatically correct. The important part is getting things out of your head and on paper.

2. Write like no one will ever read it - that will free you to write what you really feel/think with no judgment.

3. Decide if you prefer to journal by writing in a notebook or by doing it on the notes app on your computer or using an app like Evernote.

4. Block out intentional time to do it. Make it a habit to journal for 10 minutes at the end of a day or first thing in the morning.

5. Sometimes it helps to have a sample framework when you are journaling about something specific. An example from my own life when I was working on boundaries would look something like this: I took a particular situation when someone started pushing me past my limits, so I stopped and set firm boundaries. Then I reflected on it so I could anchor it in my brain for next time and gain insight from that experience. I got a piece of paper and wrote 3 sections:
    a) <u>Clues</u>: Here I bulleted all the clues that my boundaries were about to be stepped on.
    b) <u>Positive actions I took:</u> Here I bulleted all the positive actions I took when I realized what my clues were showing me.
    c) <u>How it felt</u>: Here I bulleted how it felt to enforce and stick with my boundaries. Things like feeling empowered, and that it felt fulfilling to stand up for myself, and not let myself be taken advantage of, or how making the decision brought an immediate end to any confusion or chaos I felt.

Checklist

- ☐ Reflective journaling doesn't have to sound like middle school drama.
- ☐ Reflective is the key part of journaling. Take your experience and gain insight from it to grow and learn.
- ☐ It allows you to get your feelings on paper and get to the bottom of what's really going on in a situation by exploring and articulating the deeper-level emotions.
- ☐ When you write it down and reflect, no experience is ever wasted.
- ☐ Do not overthink it or try to write perfectly. Write like no one will ever read it.
- ☐ Decide if you prefer to journal with pen and paper or on a computer app.
- ☐ Block out intentional time to do it.
- ☐ Use a framework or reflective journaling questions if that helps. *The quick-reference guide with all of the self-coaching questions from this book is a great place to start. Download your free copy at www.lifehacksforhardtimes.com.

Self-Coaching Questions

- ✓ What could I do differently next time?
- ✓ What is one thing I learned about myself through this situation?
- ✓ How did it feel to stand in my power and speak my truth?

CHAPTER 23

REFUELING STATIONS FOR YOUR LIFE

You Can't Pour From an Empty Cup

"When you recover or discover something that nourishes your soul and brings joy, care enough about yourself to make room for it in your life." - Jean Shinoda Bolen

As I was walking through the mall, my phone rang, and on the other end I heard the words from my husband at the time that would forever change the trajectory of my life. "I've thought about things, and I've decided I don't want to make our marriage work. I'm filing for divorce." I told him, "Okay, I'll wait for the papers." You may be wondering why I had such a passive response. For years, I fought for our marriage, tried to make it work, and desperately begged him to step up to the plate and fight for our marriage as well. It was at the end of that several-year fight that I finally gave him the ultimatum. I am leaving this house and giving you space and time to decide if you want to take initiative and make this work or not. A couple of weeks after I left, that was the phone call I received. Right or wrong - I had no more fight left in me if he wasn't willing.

The life I had spent the last several years building was being torn down before my eyes, and there was no stopping it. But I knew in the midst of all the emotions, all the change, and all the stress, I had to be able to find ways to feed my soul, or I would burn out in the process. I also knew that I had no desire or intention to be single for the rest of my life. I would have to get myself back out on the dating scene at some point, so I better take care of myself.

In those months of guilt, shame, and grief, I incorporated things into my life that fed my soul in the midst of it all. I took on rollerblading and spent hours at the park skating. I went to the humane society and adopted a cat, whom I loved for the 17 years following. He gave me companionship and made me laugh in the midst of my tears. I booked a mission trip to Mexico, took the orphanage kids to the beach for the day, and bought them school uniforms and supplies. I researched and started my own professional organizing business.

Friends, it's so important that we all have Refueling Stations in our lives. These are people, places, hobbies, songs, Bible verses, quotes, stories, and so on that we can go to that will fill us up. It's even more important that we have these stations when we are going through hard times. They are critical to our mental health and even our survival in some cases.

Here's what I've learned about Refueling Stations for my life:

> **Refueling stations refuel you physically, mentally, spiritually, and emotionally.** To be a refueling station in your life it must be something or someone who fills you up in at least one of those 4 areas. Some examples are hobbies you love to do, books you love to read, or songs that inspire you in the midst of pain. *A comprehensive list of refueling stations is in the bonus section of downloads at www.lifehacksforhardtimes.com.

➤ **Why do you need them?**
- o As we'll talk about in the Self-Care Chapter 24, you can't run on empty. Knowing what these stations are in your life allows you to make sure you don't run out of gas.
- o You can keep them in your "back pocket", so when you are feeling tapped out, you know immediately where to go to get filled back up. For example, when I'm feeling overwhelmed, I know I need to get outside in nature, even for a few minutes, and it will instantly allow me to relax.
- o Helps you be intentional about not always giving out without stopping and refueling yourself, and these stations allow you to know exactly how to do that.

➤ **Don't wait until you are burned out to create them.** If you don't have these written down and easily accessible in your life, you need to find and create them before you hit a wall. The moment of feeling burnt out is not the time to try to figure out what to do about it.

How To Get It:

1. Download the worksheet in the bonus section and fill in the blanks for each of the sections. If there is a section that you have no answers for, then spend some time exploring options and finding what fills you up. For example, if you have no hobbies and don't even know what to do for fun or recreation, start trying things you think you may enjoy, and eventually, you'll find the things that bring you joy. But you must start trying different things.

2. Pay attention to when you have certain energy drops, and why those may be happening. When you notice those signs of energy drops, be intentional about incorporating at least one of the refueling stations into your day immediately.

3. To be proactive about this, I would encourage you to not put back-to-back things in your day that drain your energy. Make sure if you have a 2-hour meeting today that you know is going to tap you out, that after that meeting, you incorporate something from your

refueling stations to fill you back up. That way, you don't even allow yourself to get too empty and hit a wall.

Checklist

- ☐ Refueling stations are people or things that refuel you physically, mentally, emotionally, or spiritually.
- ☐ They are things that bring joy and positive energy to your life.
- ☐ You need them in your life because you can't run on empty.
- ☐ When you start feeling overwhelmed or tapped out, you can immediately tap into these stations and refuel your body, mind, and spirit.
- ☐ Don't wait until you are burnt out to create them.
- ☐ Download the list in the Free Resources section and be intentional about filling it out and keeping it somewhere you can easily reference it - maybe in a journal or notebook, maybe the notes app on your phone, or maybe a sheet taped to your bedroom mirror.
- ☐ Pay attention when you have energy drops, and use the refueling stations as a way to refill almost immediately before you run out of gas.
- ☐ Be proactive to not put back-to-back things in your schedule all day that drain your energy, without inserting refueling stations in between.

Self-Coaching Questions

- ✓ What brings me joy?
- ✓ What or who is draining my energy right now?
- ✓ Am I running on empty, and do I need to be intentional about stopping to fill up?
- ✓ When am I at my best?
- ✓ How would I like to feel?

CHAPTER 24

SELF-CARE

Put Your Oxygen Mask on First

"Self-care is giving the world the best of you, instead of the what's left of you."

- Katie Reed

I 'll never forget the day I found myself standing in the kitchen with my smartphone in my hand, solving what I felt like were all the world's problems. I had already sent more messages and emails than I could count, made several phone calls, and I was knocking things out. Everyone was loving Christie that day because she was solving their problems.

Then it hit me...It was about 11:30am. The only thing I had done for myself so far that morning was shower. I was literally standing in my kitchen in my bra and underwear (if you show up at my house unannounced, that's on you). I hadn't done my hair, my makeup, nor had I eaten or drank anything that morning. I was in total firefighter mode, taking care of the urgent, but not the important. Yes, there is a difference.

That day, I made a decision that if I didn't start taking care of myself first, I was going to be no good to anyone because I was going to burn out, and when I did, there was no guarantee I would recover. That was the day I made the decision that my phone has its home on my office desk and not in my bedroom. It was also the day I made the decision that until I have taken care of myself and my family in the mornings, I don't look at my phone. Until I've got my morning walk or run in, eaten a healthy breakfast, and am totally ready for the day - no one gets any part of me, other than the people in my household.

This allows me to show up for the world at my best - fully engaged, focused on my priorities, and living my purpose.

When we are going through hard and stressful times, it is even more imperative that we take care of ourselves. We are using more mental, emotional, and physical energy during those times. Therefore, we must stop and fill up or we won't make it through, and if we don't, there won't be anything left of us on the other side.

This chapter is by no means a complete look at self-care; there are many books written on the issue. If this is an area of struggle for you, I would encourage you to find someone you trust and respect on the topic, and go learn more about it. I wanted to at least touch on it in this book because it should be a permanent tool in your toolbox of life hacks.

Here's what I've learned about Self-Care:

> **Self-care isn't selfish.** There are misconceptions and extremes about self-care. Self-care doesn't mean you are some diva who walks around town all day with your fur leopard coat and Gucci purse, going from salon to salon getting pampered all day, having everyone wait on you while looking at the rest of the world like they haven't arrived. That's self-absorption. Self-care also isn't having what I would call martyr syndrome. You know the person who never takes care of themselves because their kids, their family, and the world needs all of them to keep going. The mom who doesn't even have

time to shower or fix her hair because her kids require 24-hour attention. That is not selflessness - that is in its own way self-absorption and codependency (that's another book). When you fly, what do they tell you about the oxygen mask? Put yours on first if there is an emergency so you can breathe to help others. Healthy self-care is stewarding your body, soul, and spirit so you can show up to the world and live your purpose without sacrificing yourself in the process.

➤ **You can't run on empty.** If I decide to take a road trip from California to New York, and as I'm driving across the country, I notice my gas gauge is going down, but I think, "I don't have time to fill up, I need to get there faster, I have too much to do, and I just can't stop and fill up with gas," you know exactly what's going to happen. I'm going to be stranded along the highway out of gas; then it's going to take me longer AND cost me more to get to my destination because I wouldn't take 10 minutes, get off at an exit, and fill the car up with gas. Self-care is the same way. Now, if I'm doing that same road trip with a U-Haul hauling my car, I'm going to burn through gas faster and have to stop more often because it's requiring more gas to carry all that weight. That's how it is when we are going through hard or stressful times; we require MORE self-care, more often. You may require more sleep in certain seasons of your life. You may not be able to get as much done in a day during a season. You may not be able to keep up with as many relationships. You may have to invest more in your physical health than in other seasons. But friends, you must take care of YOU, or you will run out of gas and be forced to.

➤ **Our ego needs to be replenished from hard time to hard time.** First off, let me clarify the term ego because I know that word has a negative connotation. Simply put, it means one's sense of self-worth. We usually view it in the exaggerated term where it becomes conceit. But at its core, ego is something we all have, and it's not a bad thing. Having a reasonable sense of your own worth is not a sin or selfishness! When you are going through hard times, your ego gets depleted, and it's important that you build it back up before you run out of gas, as I stated in point #2 above.

How to get it:

1. Decide that taking care of yourself is not selfish, and that you are worth it. If this is a struggle for you, then you need to dive into this topic more and ask yourself some tough questions like, "Why don't I feel worthy of taking care of me?"

2. Make a commitment that you are going to prioritize self-care in your life and make that commitment non-negotiable. You get to decide what you need to take care of yourself, no one else.

3. Put it on your calendar. The best way I have found to prioritize self-care and make a commitment to yourself is to put it on your calendar and treat it like any other appointment. You wouldn't just bump your dentist appointment if a friend asked you to walk their dog; you would tell them you have another appointment. The same is true for your self-care appointments. Put them on the calendar and KEEP THEM.

4. If you have no idea what you even need to take care of yourself, ask yourself the question, "What do I need most right now?"

5. Refer back to your Refueling Centers and "what brings you joy" lists to help identify ways you can fill yourself back up.

Checklist

- ☐ Self-care isn't selfish.
- ☐ You can't run on empty. It is imperative that you stop and refill yourself before you get to a place of burnout.
- ☐ When you are filled up and taking care of yourself, you can show up to the world in the best version of yourself and freely give.
- ☐ Don't forget, as you go from hard time to hard time, you will need

to replenish your ego. Sometimes that may look like a night off, sometimes it's a vacation, sometimes it's a 30-minute walk.

- ☐ Make a commitment to yourself that you are going to take care of YOU.
- ☐ Put your own self-care on your calendar and keep your appointments with yourself.
- ☐ What do you need most right now? You will know - remember to identify the truth - be honest with yourself.
- ☐ Keep your list of what brings you joy and your refueling centers for your life handy.

Self-Coaching Questions

- ✓ What do I need most right now?
- ✓ How would I like to feel?
- ✓ What or who is draining my energy right now?
- ✓ When am I at my best?
- ✓ What is the single, most meaningful change I can make in this area?

CHAPTER 25

SUPPORT SYSTEM

Don't Go at It Alone

"If you don't have the information you need to make wise choices, find someone

who does." - Lori Hill

We're driving down the winding back road on our way home from Wednesday night church, when Matt says to me, "Pull over and let me out - I can't handle this anymore". I happened to be driving that night, and we were fighting - which was how we operated the first 5 years of our marriage. So, I complied with his request and pulled off the berm of that winding road. As I began to slow the car down, and as we were rolling to a stop, he opened his door and jumped out. I sped back up so the door would slam itself shut, and off I went. It was only about 3 miles to our house, which in a car was no big deal. I arrived home, grabbed a drink, and went to sit on the swing out back.

A bit later, after jogging home in his church clothes, Matt arrived at the house, out of breath and still angry. So I said to him, "Are you ready to talk now?" Yes, I really said that, and it wasn't in a sweet way. I'll let you imagine his response and how the rest of the evening went.

Matt and I are complete opposites, and when we got married, he was a naive 27-year-old who didn't know much about life, and I had been through a ton in life. On the outside, I looked the best I had in years, but inside I was as broken and beat up as a stolen car in the hood. Neither of us had any idea what a healthy version of each other looked like, let alone what a healthy relationship looked like. We struggled so hard for years. With my past of broken and unhealthy relationships, looking for attention in all the wrong places, being taken advantage of by anyone and everyone, and trusting no one at that point, I was an emotional mess. With his immaturity, past of pornography and video game addiction, and no drive for life, our marriage was truly headed for divorce many times.

Thankfully, the story didn't end there because, while we did just about everything wrong, the one thing we did right was decide to fight to make this work. We knew if we were going to make it work, we needed to bring someone alongside us to help. We had two couples in our lives who happened to be our pastors at different seasons of our lives, and they both had great marriages. So, we got over our own pride and need to look like we had it all together, because we clearly did not, and we let them into our mess. They both helped us through some of the most crucial times of our marriage, and I truly believe if we didn't have that outside support, we wouldn't have the thriving marriage that we have today, and probably wouldn't even be married.

I'm a very independent, tough person who can fight through a lot on my own, but there have been many seasons in my life where I knew I couldn't fight and win on my own. You and I are built for human connection, and it's so important to have other people in our lives, especially when we are going through hard times. But it's important that we don't just bring anyone alongside us.

Here's what I've learned about having a Support System:

- ➢ **Having the right support system is key.** Not just anyone in your life is equipped to help you through what you are experiencing. And the wrong support system can cause more harm than good. There would have been a lot of people in my life, when I was struggling so badly in my marriage, who would have told me to just divorce Matt and move on with my life. There also would have been a lot of people in my life who would not have been qualified to support us through that time. When your marriage is struggling, you don't want someone who has been divorced 4 times, and currently single, giving you marriage advice. Just like you don't want someone who has gone bankrupt and is struggling financially to help you invest and manage your money. You need support, but you need the right support. The best way to do this is to find someone who has walked a similar path like you are on, and has overcome to help you in that area. They don't need to have every area of their life in check - most people don't. But don't go hire a 350 lb. health coach who hasn't exercised since they were 13. If you find someone who has a thriving marriage but can't manage their money - that doesn't matter to you - you aren't asking them for money advice - you want their marriage wisdom.

- ➢ **You'll need different support for different seasons.** Just because someone supported you in a season or area of your life, doesn't mean they'll be the right support for you now. People change and grow (or they don't grow). Seasons of your life change, so the support and relationships that worked 20 years ago may not work now. For me personally, my biggest support in most areas of my life has come from hiring personal or business coaches. These coaches have looked different through the different seasons of my life and business, but they've been just who I needed for the season of life I was in.

- ➢ **You must be proactive in finding support.** Someone isn't going to show up at your door with a messenger bag and say, "Give me your hand, let me help you through this hard time." It's just not going to happen friends. Finding the right support for the season you are in requires INTENTIONAL effort on your part. I know that when you are in a hard time, it's exhausting to think about having to find the right person to help you, but you must search them out. And you must be willing to invest in yourself. As I said, the majority of my support over my lifetime has been from PAID life or business coaches. But it was worth every penny I invested, 10 times over.

> **Establish expectations with your support system.** Once you do find the right support, establishing proper expectations is important. You need to establish what you are expecting and what they are willing or capable of giving. Set boundaries both ways. Remember, this person isn't your savior, they are your support. They aren't going to swoop in like Batman and save you - that only happens in the movies. But they can be a great listener, encourager, and guide. And, knowing you aren't alone in your mess is sometimes one of the greatest comforts you can have.

How to get it:

1. Determine where you are AND where you are going in this hard place. If you are struggling with your marriage and want to make it work OR if you are struggling with your marriage and want to file for divorce and make sure you are treated fairly in the process - the support system looks totally different based on your situation. So you must first IDENTIFY THE TRUTH of your situation (Chapter 1).

2. Proactively find someone who has walked the path. You can also ask friends, family members, or trusted acquaintances if they know someone who can help with whatever you are dealing with.

3. If you are hiring a professional, please make sure they either have personal experience in the area you are struggling with OR they have helped other people overcome in those areas.

4. Be willing to invest in your future, yourself, your marriage, your parenting, your business, your health - whatever area you are going through a hard time in. If you had a broken arm, you wouldn't just ask some random friend to cast it up for you so you didn't have to pay a doctor. You would go get your arm fixed right by someone who knows what they are doing. You are worth investing in. If you need to hire someone - then hire them. It is an INVESTMENT that (if you hire the right person) will pay you back more times than you can count.

5. Clearly communicate your expectations and needs with your support system. Do not expect them to read your mind.

Checklist

- ☐ Having the right support system is key, don't let just anyone into your struggle.
- ☐ Determine where you are and where you want to go - so you know WHO to bring alongside you.
- ☐ Find someone who has walked the path you are on OR has helped other people walk that path.
- ☐ Your support will look different for different seasons of your life.
- ☐ You must be proactive and intentional about finding the right support system. No one is just going to show up at your door with a magic wand.
- ☐ Be willing to invest your time, energy, and resources into your support. They are bringing something to the table to add value to your life, and you need to bring something to the table. You'll get far better results that way.
- ☐ Clearly communicate expectations and establish boundaries with your support, whether they are volunteer or paid. Don't skip this step.

Self-Coaching Questions

✓ Where am I struggling?
✓ Where do I want to be in this area of my life?
✓ What do I most hope to accomplish by bringing this coach, therapist, friend, or guide into my life?
✓ Who do I know that has walked a similar path and found
✓ healing, wholeness, and is thriving in this area of life?

CHAPTER 26

ADD VALUE

Make Others Better in the Midst of Your Own Struggle

"The best way to add value to yourself is by adding value to other people."

- John C. Maxwell

A month after Matt resigned from his job, and we were working on crawling out of our mess, we decided to get some RACK (Random Acts of Christmas Kindness) cards printed and tape them to people's cars in the parking lots of churches and stores. We would add candy bars or Starbucks gift cards or other things to them, just to brighten someone's day. We were deep in our struggle, living on a home equity loan, and had no idea what the future held, but it was important that we continued to give in the midst of it all.

Another time I'll never forget - I was standing in the kitchen where we were staying in our friends' house in Wisconsin. The girls had gone over to the neighbors to help her rake leaves, and they came running back into the house, enthusiastically wanting to bake Miss Denise a fall dessert. What our kids didn't know at that moment was that we were struggling badly financially. My mom was actually helping us pay for groceries just so we could eat, so making the neighbor a dessert at that moment in our life was a huge sacrifice. But I also knew that there was no way I was going to deny my kids an opportunity to give or add value to someone else even in the midst of our own struggle. So they baked a delicious pumpkin dessert that day and took it over for Miss Denise and her husband to enjoy after a long day of yard work.

Here's the thing. I'm not telling you these stories so you can ooh and aah over what amazing people we are, or anything of the sort. But I am making a point here on how important it is that we add value to others as a way of life…even in the hard times. My heart behind this chapter is also not one of the mindsets that says, "There are people struggling worse than you in third world countries, so get over yourself." That is the last thing I would ever say to someone. I'm not undermining your struggles, and I'm not undermining my own struggles I've had, or currently have in any way by writing this chapter. However, I know the power of giving and adding value to others in the midst of my own storm. It is something I don't ever lose sight of, no matter how bad I have it.

Here's what I've learned about Adding Value to others:

> ➤ There are 2 ways you can add value to others with your hard times.
>   - ○ #1 After you've been through something, you can find someone else struggling with something similar and pay it forward by helping them with the insights and tools you've gained through your own challenges. An example of this is my ability to help others who struggle with mental health challenges because I've walked that road, and I can pass on the valuable keys I've learned along the way to them, along with offering them hope that they can get to the other side.

- o #2 When you are in a hard time, it helps if you can re-focus, even if it's just for a short time, and do something for someone else who is also struggling in some way in their life.

➤ **You never know what hard times others are going through.** I was sitting on the plane headed to Florida after my divorce and the breakup of my other relationship, still healing from my own broken heart. I started talking to the girl beside me, and she shared that she was headed to Florida to meet her fiance's parents. Excited for her, I asked the next logical question - "When are you getting married?" She immediately burst into tears and through her pain muttered, "He died last week." That was not the answer I was expecting at all, but in that moment I had the opportunity to just offer a listening ear and a compassionate heart to someone who was hurting deeply. No one had any idea what was going on with her from an outside glance. Until I asked questions and got into her world, I didn't know either. Needless to say, my pain that day didn't seem as significant. She felt seen and heard that day, and it may be just what her broken heart needed.

➤ **Adding value to others gives you a fulfillment you can't find through anything else.** The satisfaction and fulfillment that comes from knowing you added value to someone else in a difficult time is a feeling I can't really describe. You just have to do it, and experience it for yourself.

How To Get It:

1. Be intentional about looking up from your own misery and hard time, even for a moment, and finding someone else going through something, and go add value to them. It doesn't have to be some grand gesture. Sometimes the smallest acts of kindness can have the greatest impact.

2. Identify what hard times you have gone through and have come out better on the other side. Then find someone you can pay it forward with and help them with a similar situation. Don't waste the pain you walked through.

3. Stop and recognize how you feel when you add value to someone else. Let yourself soak in the feelings and experience.

Checklist

☐ Adding value to others is a way of life that will enrich your life, even in your hard times.

☐ You can add value to others amidst your own struggle, and you can find ways you can pay it forward to others based on the keys you've learned through your own hard times.

☐ You never know what others are going through. Ask questions and get into their world, they'll tell you if you ask.

☐ Adding value to others gives you a sense of fulfillment you won't find through anything else.

☐ Be intentional about adding value to others...especially when you are struggling yourself.

☐ Use your past experiences to pay it forward to someone else. Don't waste the pain you've already been through.

☐ Recognize how it feels to add value to others.

Self-Coaching Questions

- ✓ How could you raise the bar and embrace a higher standard in this area?
- ✓ How is someone else's life better when they cross your path?
- ✓ Who in my life can I add value to this week?

CHAPTER 27

CELEBRATE SMALL WINS

Give Yourself a High-Five

"Focus on progress not perfection." - Bill Phillips

I walked out onto the volleyball court in my bright orange and turquoise matching size 2 Nike shorts and t-shirt, hair pulled up in a ponytail, nails freshly manicured - boy did I look great!…on the outside. Not to mention the train wreck that I was on the inside, but that's another story. As I mentioned before, when I went through my divorce, I knew I had to get back out on the dating playing field, so I was at the skinniest and fittest I ever was in my life. Then I got re-married and had my first child, so size 2's turned into 8's. Then I was pregnant with the second child and started the battle for my mental and physical health. Blood sugar issues and anxiety ruled my life, and I gained more weight than I ever had in my life. Then came a miscarriage, another pregnancy, and more years of my body and my mind being under complete stress and turmoil. I was so overweight, my hair was lifeless, and my skin was dull. By this time I had racked up more stretch marks than I cared to count, and my weight loved to hang out in my mid-section, to which people would ask me while holding my newborn baby if I was pregnant again. Just a side note - don't ever do that to someone. What once was a confident, vibrant, fit young woman was now an overweight, stressed out, "insecure in her body" woman who spent her days fighting for her life.

Then came the moment I turned the corner on my mental health battle for good and started heading toward life and freedom. But you know what, I was still overweight, my stomach still liked to hold my weight, my stretch marks were still going strong, and the stress I had put my body under for years was still showing up all over my body. But my first priority wasn't how good I looked in a swimsuit; it was being able to function for a day without debilitating panic and anxiety. Then it was being able to actually sleep through the night for the first time in years. Then it was being able to actually care enough to be able to get up every day, shower, fix my lifeless hair, and throw on some makeup. Then came the time when the desire grew to find someone to show me how to do my makeup and take it up a notch. Then came the day it was time to find someone who could give me a new haircut. Then I had the energy to start exercising again and begin to build up my body. Then I got to the point where I realized getting back a body that I was confident and proud of may take some time and a lot of work, but in the meantime, I need to appreciate what I have and take care of it the best I can. As I drove through the car wash, I watched a guy vacuuming out his car, while his wife sat in the passenger seat. He walked around to her side and opened the door, and I realized why she was sitting there. She was an amputee. At that moment a huge wave of conviction, coupled with gratefulness, flooded my heart as I realized that here I am feeling sad about the 2 varicose veins on my leg and the countless stretch marks, when there is a lady sitting there who would love to just have legs, no matter what size they were. That was the moment I decided I was going to start appreciating the body I had while taking care of it and moving towards my health goals. I also realized that day that I needed to start celebrating my wins every step of the way, because even though I sit here today writing this book with size 12 pants on and a 44-year-old body, 8 years ago I couldn't even get out of bed. As I sit here in these size 12 jeans, I realize the broken glass I've crawled over to get where I am, and it's time I start celebrating this body and everything that comes with it and stop sitting around waiting to celebrate until I'm on the cover of a swim magazine (which isn't ever going to happen, by the way!).

Friends, you and I must stop and celebrate our small wins along the way! Some days no one else will be standing alongside the track cheering you - so you must cheer yourself on!

Here's what I've learned about Celebrating the Small Wins:

➢ **You must be intentional about pausing and celebrating.** If you are an overachiever, like me, your tendency will be to just keep pushing yourself and moving at lightning speed, never taking the time to stop and acknowledge what you've done or how far you've come. You'll just keep setting the bar higher and higher and keep going. Instead of looking at everything you still have to do and still haven't accomplished, pause for a moment and look at what you have accomplished or what you have walked through.

➢ **You will burn out if you go from goal to goal.** I learned this from coach, Valorie Burton, if you keep going from goal to goal without refueling yourself and acknowledging your wins, you will burn out. It takes a tremendous amount of that ego we talked about and resilience to push through hard times. So when you keep acting like the finish line of one hard time is the start of the next hard time and don't stop to refuel and celebrate, you start the next hard time with half a tank of gas, and you will eventually run out of gas and burn out.

➢ **Be intentional about acknowledging progress.** It's so easy when you are in a hard time to just focus on the hard time and feel like you aren't getting anywhere, instead of acknowledging all the progress you've made. Just like I told you in my story - I could look in the mirror and think, "Boy, I'm still in my size 12 jeans, this stomach still isn't perfectly flat yet, and these stretch marks - ugh." But when I look back at how this same girl looked and functioned years earlier and realize the progress, it's a whole new perspective. I'm not where I want to be with my body, but I'm also not where I used to be.

➤ **Acknowledging anchors positive neurons in your brain.** Our brain quickly and easily fires negative neurons, as you know. It takes more effort for the positive neurons to fire in our brain. So when we are intentional about acknowledging and even writing these wins down (see Reflective Journaling Chapter 22), it helps us to keep our perspective and not lose sight of the vision we have on the other side of our hard time.

How To Get It:

1. Ask yourself how you can actually measure the progress you are making through your hard time. What checkpoints can you put in place? Just like someone running a marathon would have mile markers to know where they are in the journey, set up mile markers for yourself so you can measure your progress. Then stop at those mile markers and celebrate.

2. Stop or pause and celebrate. Every win doesn't mean you need to take a 7-day Alaskan cruise, it could be as simple as a high-five with your spouse! Go grab a coffee at your favorite coffee shop and take an hour to celebrate. Go out to dinner! Sometimes I reward myself with a houseplant. The point is, you need to acknowledge it - how you do it is up to you.

3. Journal your successes. There is power in writing your wins down. It anchors positive neurons in your brain and will encourage you when you go back and reflect on your wins. Refer back to Chapter 22 on Reflective Journaling.

    BONUS TIP: My coach encouraged me to get a brag journal. Anytime I get a nice message from someone, someone encourages me in some way or sends me a note - I write these things in this journal. On my rough days, I can refer back to that journal and encourage myself through the powerful, positive words others have spoken into my life.

4. Share it with a friend. Find the people in your life who will celebrate with you! Not the negative Nellies or the envious Evas, but find the people who will celebrate with you and share your progress with them! Maybe you are working on setting boundaries in a toxic relationship and you just had a huge win today - share it with a friend who knows your struggles and will cheer you on!

Checklist

- ☐ You must be intentional about pausing and celebrating small wins during your hard time.
- ☐ If you keep going from goal to goal or hard time to hard time without stopping to celebrate and refuel, you will burn out.
- ☐ Be intentional about acknowledging the progress you have made, even though you aren't where you want to be - you aren't where you used to be either.
- ☐ Acknowledging and writing down wins anchors positive neurons in your brain.
- ☐ Set up checkpoints to celebrate and measure your wins.
- ☐ Then stop at those checkpoints and celebrate in some way - big or small.
- ☐ Journal your successes so you can refer back to them to encourage you through future hard times.
- ☐ Share your wins with a friend who will celebrate with you!

Self-Coaching Questions

- ✓ What do I need to stop and acknowledge right now during my current hard time?
- ✓ What ways can I celebrate my small wins?
- ✓ Who is safe to share my wins with?
- ✓ How do I want to celebrate this milestone?

CONCLUSION

"One small step in the right direction can be the biggest step of your life."

- Anonymous

When I was young, I envisioned what my life would look like. But in that vision, I didn't see divorce, infertility, mental illness, financial struggles, or toxic relationships. I didn't see any of that, but I also don't regret anything I've walked through. I know none of it was wasted, and all of it was used for a bigger purpose, even the stupid, incredibly wrong things I have done.

Maybe your life hasn't played out the way you thought it would either, whether by your choice or unfortunate circumstances. Either way, friend, you have a choice on how it affects you and what you do with the hard things you went through. It is my hope and prayer that you don't continue to suffer through your struggles. But instead, you take the tools in this book, and from today forward, you make the bold choice to build something incredible out of the brokenness you have been through or are currently in.

If you read this book, it is not an accident. It is a gift for you. A gift that hopefully infuses you with hope, encouragement, and inspiration. A gift that gives you the insight and how-to's to change your life one right step at a time. A gift that can possibly change the trajectory of your life if you do something with it.

One thing I know for sure is that you were created with a purpose. You have unique strengths, talents, and capabilities that the world needs. Don't let one more day go by without being intentional about your life and living out your God-given purpose on this earth. It's YOUR time!

Remember, every day is a chance to change your life. I'm right there with you in this journey called life, cheering you on while jumping my own hurdles!

All the best, *Christie*

P.S. Your stories inspire me! My team and I would love to hear your story of overcoming your own obstacles, and the impact you were able to have on your world because of it. Email us at hello@maxpotential.coach.